Reading
Connections 1

From Academic Success to Everyday Fluency

Andrew E. Bennett

HEINLE
CENGAGE Learning™

Australia • Brazil • Japan • Korea • Mexico • Singapore • Spain • United Kingdom • United States

HEINLE
CENGAGE Learning

Reading Connections 1:
From Academic Success to Everyday Fluency
Andrew E. Bennett

Publisher, the Americas, Global, and Dictionaries:
Sherrise Roehr
Acquisitions Editor: Tom Jefferies
Senior Development Editor: Yeny Kim
Director of US Marketing: Jim McDonough
Senior Product Marketing Manager: Katie Kelley
Academic Marketing Manager: Caitlin Driscoll
Director of Global Marketing: Ian Martin
Director of Content and Media Production:
Michael Burggren
Senior Content Product Manager:
Maryellen E. Killeen
Senior Print Buyer: Mary Beth Hennebury

Images: All images: (c) istockphoto.com except pp. 37, 38, 55, 56: (c) Andrew E. Bennett

For product information and technology assistance, contact us at
Cengage Learning Customer & Sales Support, 1-800-354-9706

For permission to use material from this text or product, submit all requests online at **www.cengage.com/permissions**
Further permissions questions can be emailed to
permissionrequest@cengage.com

ISBN-13: 978-1-111-34857-1
ISBN-10: 1-111-34857-X

Heinle
20 Channel Center Street
Boston, MA 02210
USA

Cengage Learning is a leading provider of customized learning solutions with office locations around the globe, including Singapore, the United Kingdom, Australia, Mexico, Brazil and Japan. Locate your local office at
international.cengage.com/region

Cengage Learning products are represented in Canada by Nelson Education, Ltd.

Visit Heinle online at **elt.heinle.com**
Visit our corporate website at **www.cengage.com**

Printed in Canada
1 2 3 4 5 6 7 14 13 12 11 10

Contents

Introduction

Reading Connections 1 Overview

Reading Connections 1 combines integrated skill building and interesting content. The book contains 20 units based on a variety of modern topics. At the core of each unit is a reading passage, with interconnected vocabulary, listening, speaking, grammar, and writing activities. This comprehensive method allows students' English to rapidly improve. At the same time, engaging topics keep students interested and motivated while they learn.

Following are the features found in each unit of *Reading Connections 1*.

Pre-Reading Questions

This exercise includes three simple questions about the topic. It's designed to get students to start thinking about the topic for a few minutes. The exercise can be done in pairs, or the entire class can discuss the questions together.

Consider the Topic

This pre-reading exercise gives each student a chance to register his or her opinion about three statements related to the topic. The exercise helps make students more active and interested learners.

Reading Passage

The core component of each unit is an article about a modern topic. The topics are from a wide range of fields, including technology, health, science, modern lifestyles, sports, the environment, and more. This variety reflects the wide range of our daily literacy experiences and the breadth of issues facing us in the 21st century.

Each article in *Reading Connections 1* is about 200 words long. The vocabulary and grammar are carefully controlled, to improve comprehension and allow for focused instruction. The unit's target vocabulary words and phrases (which are tested in the Vocabulary Building and Phrase Building exercises) are bolded for easy reference.

Above the article is an audio CD icon. Next to it is a track number, indicating the track on the audio CD where students can listen to a recording of the article. Beneath the article is a glossary with definitions of the article's challenging words and phrases. The definitions are written in simplified English.

Questions about the Reading

There are five multiple choice comprehension questions. A wide variety of question types are used, including main idea, detail, vocabulary in context, and more.

Writing about the Article

This exercise gives students a chance to write short responses to questions about the article. To make things easier, the first few words of each answer are given. Each answer should be one sentence long.

Vocabulary Building

In this exercise, the unit's eight target vocabulary words are tested. The target words were selected for their usefulness and frequency of use. They are the words students are going to use and encounter over and over when speaking, reading, and writing English.

Phrase Building

This exercise tests the unit's three target phrases. It is in a "cloze passage" format. Phrases should be used only once, and students should make sure to use the correct word form. Note that there are four phrases but only three blanks. The extra phrase is there to reduce the impact of guessing.

Grammar Exercise

This exercise focuses on important grammar skills. It is designed to strengthen students' proficiency in reading and writing key language structures. Each exercise is based on a structure found in the unit's Reading Passage.

Listening Exercise

The three questions in this exercise are based on a short conversation (about 50 words long) between two people. The conversation, which is recorded on the audio CD, is related to the unit's topic. (The track number is written next to the audio CD icon.) Not only is this exercise good practice for strengthening general listening skills, but it's also excellent practice for tests such as TOEIC and TOEFL.

Listening Activity

This activity is based on a short talk (about 50 words long). Each talk, which is related to the unit's topic, is recorded on the audio CD. (The track number is written next to the audio CD icon.) A variety of talk types are used, including information announcements, advertisements, introductions, and others. This activity gives students practice listening for key details, just as they would in the real world.

Discussion Questions

Now it's time for students to discuss questions related to the unit's topic. As they've already read an article and listened to a conversation and short talk about the topic (in addition to doing many other exercises), it's time for students to share their own ideas. The three questions in this exercise can be discussed in pairs, or the class can discuss the questions together.

Discussion Activity

This is the final exercise in each unit. Groups of classmates work together on a discussion activity. Simple directions for the activity are given, and a model example is provided to help students start talking.

Reading Connections **Program Overview**

Reading Connections is a NEW five-level series designed to develop the language and fluency necessary for success in real world and academic settings. The following pages highlight and explain key features of the *Reading Connections* program.

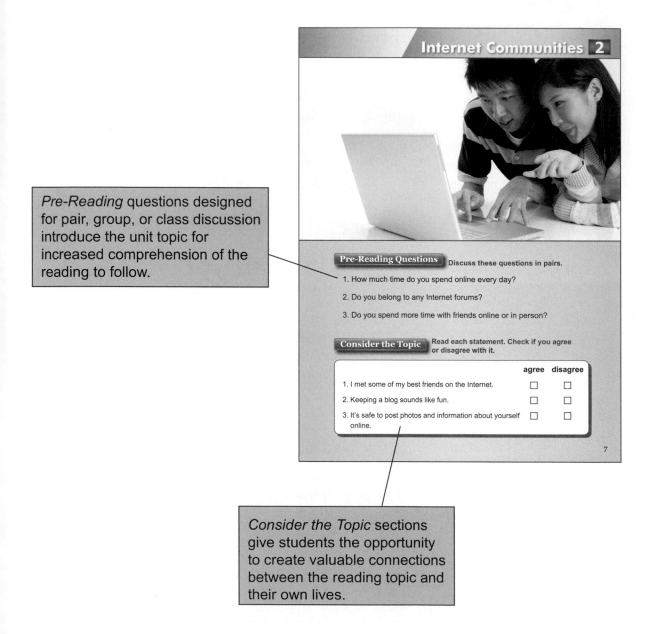

Pre-Reading questions designed for pair, group, or class discussion introduce the unit topic for increased comprehension of the reading to follow.

Consider the Topic sections give students the opportunity to create valuable connections between the reading topic and their own lives.

Unique and engaging readings, including contemporary topics such as **space tourism** and **speed dating**, connect academic content to real world fluency.

Questions about the Reading sections in every unit assess student comprehension of the passage while teaching valuable reading skills such as finding the main idea, looking for detail, learning vocabulary in context, and making inferences. Perfect for **critical thinking** practice!

Reading Passage · Track 4

1   At its heart, the Internet is about communication. Most people use the Net to meet new friends and **stay in touch** with old ones. Over the years, whole new communities have grown online. For millions of people, belonging to an Internet community is very important to
5   their lives.

Since the Internet's early years, many websites have **included** forums. People join forums to **discuss hobbies** and subjects which interest them. Besides posting public **messages**, **members** can **contact** friends through PMs (**private** messages).

10   In the mid-2000s, "social networking" sites like MySpace and Facebook grew very quickly. On these sites, members each have a page to introduce themselves
15   and blog about their lives. Photos, music, and videos can be added. And, people can leave comments on their friends' pages.

These sites are very popular. MySpace has more than 100 million
20   members. Many people spend several hours a day on the site. Updating a blog and **keeping up with** friends' pages takes a lot of time!

That worries some people. Is it **healthy** to spend so much time online? There are also questions about safety. What kinds of details
25   should people post about their lives? These are not easy questions, and we're still **figuring out** the answers.

---
¹ communication – speaking with and writing to people
³ community – group of people who spend a lot of time together
¹¹ networking – bringing people together and making new friends
²¹ update – add new information

8

Questions about the Reading   Choose the best answer.

1. ( ) According to the article, what is key to the Internet?
 (A) Allowing people to contact one another
 (B) Making it easy to buy whatever you want
 (C) Reading the latest news right after it happens
 (D) Learning about new hobbies and subjects

2. ( ) What does the article suggest about Internet forums?
 (A) They have only just become popular over the last year.
 (B) They are a part of very few websites.
 (C) They include public and private ways to communicate.
 (D) They are usually visited by people at work.

3. ( ) What is NOT something people can do on Facebook?
 (A) Look for jobs
 (B) Write about daily activities
 (C) Upload personal photos
 (D) Add songs to a page

4. ( ) Why are some people worried about MySpace?
 (A) The site owners make people post personal details.
 (B) It is more popular than Facebook.
 (C) Members sometimes spend a lot of time on the site.
 (D) Not enough people have joined up.

5. ( ) What does the phrase *belonging to* in line 4 mean?
 (A) owning something
 (B) being part of
 (C) making sure of
 (D) finding out about

Writing about the Article   Answer each question based on the article.

1. What do people discuss on forums?
 People write about   .

2. On social networking sites, what can people do on friends' pages?
 People can leave   .

3. How many members does MySpace have?
 The website has   .

9

Writing about the Article activities ask students to write short answers in complete sentences, assessing reading comprehension while practicing writing skills.

Vocabulary Building exercises test the unit's target vocabulary in exercises designed both to assess comprehension and apply high-frequency terms to meaningful contexts.

Grammar Exercise sections provide practice in a target grammatical structure introduced in the reading passage to enhance overall comprehension and provide students with the skills necessary to read, write, and speak appropriately.

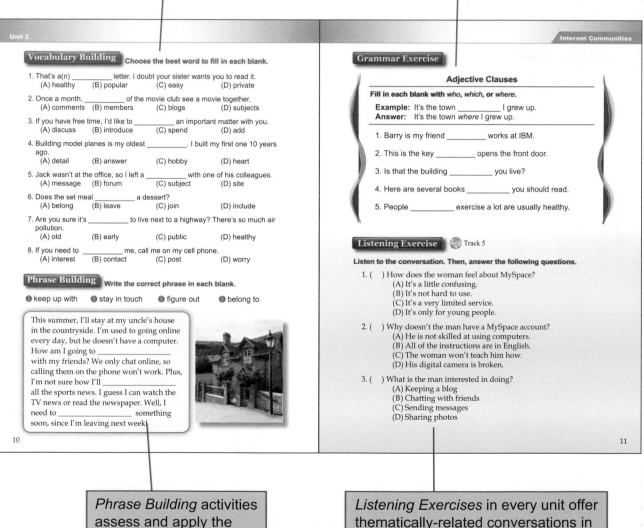

Unit 2

Internet Communities

Vocabulary Building
Choose the best word to fill in each blank.

1. That's a(n) _____ letter. I doubt your sister wants you to read it.
   (A) healthy   (B) popular   (C) easy   (D) private

2. Once a month, _____ of the movie club see a movie together.
   (A) comments   (B) members   (C) blogs   (D) subjects

3. If you have free time, I'd like to _____ an important matter with you.
   (A) discuss   (B) introduce   (C) spend   (D) add

4. Building model planes is my oldest _____. I built my first one 10 years ago.
   (A) detail   (B) answer   (C) hobby   (D) heart

5. Jack wasn't at the office, so I left a _____ with one of his colleagues.
   (A) message   (B) forum   (C) subject   (D) site

6. Does the set meal _____ a dessert?
   (A) belong   (B) leave   (C) join   (D) include

7. Are you sure it's _____ to live next to a highway? There's so much air pollution.
   (A) old   (B) early   (C) public   (D) healthy

8. If you need to _____ me, call me on my cell phone.
   (A) interest   (B) contact   (C) post   (D) worry

Phrase Building
Write the correct phrase in each blank.

● keep up with   ● stay in touch   ● figure out   ● belong to

This summer, I'll stay at my uncle's house in the countryside. I'm used to going online every day, but he doesn't have a computer. How am I going to _____ with my friends? We only chat online, so calling them on the phone won't work. Plus, I'm not sure how I'll _____ all the sports news. I guess I can watch the TV news or read the newspaper. Well, I need to _____ something soon, since I'm leaving next week!

10

Grammar Exercise

Adjective Clauses

Fill in each blank with *who, which,* or *where*.

Example: It's the town _____ I grew up.
Answer: It's the town *where* I grew up.

1. Barry is my friend _____ works at IBM.

2. This is the key _____ opens the front door.

3. Is that the building _____ you live?

4. Here are several books _____ you should read.

5. People _____ exercise a lot are usually healthy.

Listening Exercise   Track 5

Listen to the conversation. Then, answer the following questions.

1. (   ) How does the woman feel about MySpace?
   (A) It's a little confusing.
   (B) It's not hard to use.
   (C) It's a very limited service.
   (D) It's only for young people.

2. (   ) Why doesn't the man have a MySpace account?
   (A) He is not skilled at using computers.
   (B) All of the instructions are in English.
   (C) The woman won't teach him how.
   (D) His digital camera is broken.

3. (   ) What is the man interested in doing?
   (A) Keeping a blog
   (B) Chatting with friends
   (C) Sending messages
   (D) Sharing photos

11

Phrase Building activities assess and apply the unit's target phrases in a cloze exercise.

Listening Exercises in every unit offer thematically-related conversations in MP3 format on audio CD or online that assess student comprehension for test-preparation and for building fluency.

Listening Activity sections prompt students to listen and record key details from a short talk offered in a variety of formats such as advertisements and introductions to build real-world fluency.

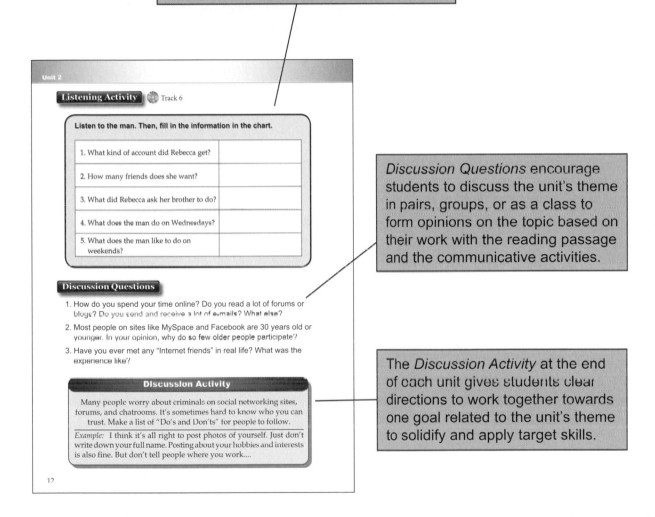

Discussion Questions encourage students to discuss the unit's theme in pairs, groups, or as a class to form opinions on the topic based on their work with the reading passage and the communicative activities.

The *Discussion Activity* at the end of each unit gives students clear directions to work together towards one goal related to the unit's theme to solidify and apply target skills.

 Audio recordings of all student book readings available in MP3 files on audio CD and FREE online at elt.heinle.com/readingconnections

Also **available**:

Assessment CD-ROM with Exam*View*® allows teachers to create tests and quizzes quickly easily!

Scope and Sequence

	Theme	Reading Skills	Grammar	Listening Exercise & Activity	Discussion Activity
1	Community	Identifying details; using vocabulary in context; making inferences	Among, Through, and About	Conversation about an upcoming event; announcement about a food drive	Organizing a volunteer event
2	The Internet	Identifying details; using vocabulary in context; recognizing suggestions	Adjective Clauses	Conversation about a social networking site; talking about an online account	Making a list of Internet do's and don'ts
3	Entertainment	Identifying the main idea and details; using vocabulary in context	Gerunds vs. Infinitives	Conversation about video games; report about a video game conference	Planning a gaming party
4	Careers	Identifying details; recognizing suggestions	Adverbs of Completion	Conversation about teleworking; announcement about a firm's teleworking policies	Holding a mini debate about teleworking
5	The Arts	Identifying details; using vocabulary in context; recognizing suggestions	Prepositions	Conversation about graffiti; report about a graffiti writing contest	Reaching a solution on the graffiti issue
6	Mobile Lifestyles	Identifying details; recognizing suggestions	The Passive Voice	Conversation about a cell phone novel; report about a cell phone novelist	Planning a cell phone novel

	Theme	Reading Skills	Grammar	Listening Exercise & Activity	Discussion Activity
7	Business	Identifying the main idea and details	Everything, Anything, and Nothing	Conversation about a store; description of a service	Planning a new boutique
8	Space	Identifying the main idea and details; using vocabulary in context	Even, Even if, and Not even	Conversation about a trip into space; report about a marriage in space	Designing a space hotel
9	Culture	Identifying the main idea and details; using vocabulary in context; recognizing suggestions	Adjectives vs. Adverbs	Conversation about a cultural taboo; advertisement for a set of instructional videos	Role playing an incident involving a cultural taboo
10	Imagination	Identifying details; using vocabulary in context; recognizing suggestions	Elsewhere, Anywhere, and Somewhere	Conversation about a toy show; advertisement for a store's sales promotion	Designing a new toy
11	Identity	Identifying the main idea and details; using vocabulary in context; recognizing implications	Present Perfect	Conversation about new neighbors; description of a class	Planning a move to another country
12	Modern Life	Identifying the main idea and details; using vocabulary in context	All, Every, and None	Conversation about a speed dating event; advertisement for an upcoming speed dating event	Learning about one's classmates

	Theme	Reading Skills	Grammar	Listening Exercise & Activity	Discussion Activity
13	World Cities	Identifying details; using vocabulary in context	Prepositions of Place	Conversation about a trip to Shanghai; report about changes in Shanghai	Planning to do business in China
14	The Environment	Identifying the main idea and details; using vocabulary in context	Modals	Conversation about hybrid cars; report about the summer storm season	Discussing running a business and protecting the environment
15	Transportation	Identifying the main idea and details; using vocabulary in context	Pronouns	Conversation about transportation options; report about high speed trains	Improving the public transportation system
16	Family	Identifying the main idea and details; recognizing suggestions	Prepositions of Time	Conversation about children; report about small families and the housing industry	Designing a campaign to raise the country's population size
17	Law and Crime	Identifying the main idea and details; using vocabulary in context; recognizing suggestions	Making Comparisons	Conversation about a credit problem; report about identity theft trends	Role playing a phone call related to identity theft
18	The Developing World	Identifying main ideas and details; using vocabulary in context; recognizing suggestions	Adverbs	Conversation about doing business in India; report about a trade office	Discussing ways to improve one's country

	Theme	Reading Skills	Grammar	Listening Exercise & Activity	Discussion Activity
19	Health	Identifying the main idea and details; using vocabulary in context	Noun Clauses	Conversation about trans fat; report about a supermarket survey	Discussing eating habits and medical responsibility
20	Science and Technology	Identifying details; using vocabulary in context; recognizing suggestions	Adjectives: -ed vs. -ing	Conversation about smart robots; report about robots and medical procedures	Imagining the future and the role robots will play

Discuss these questions in pairs.

1. What are some common types of volunteer work?

2. Have you ever worked as a volunteer? Where?

3. What are some groups in your country that help other people? How do they help?

Consider the Topic Read each statement. Check if you agree or disagree with it.

	agree	disagree
1. Many people in my country volunteer.	☐	☐
2. It's easy to find a good place to volunteer.	☐	☐
3. Everyone should spend more time volunteering.	☐	☐

Reading Passage ⊙ Track 1

1   Kim Mitchell spends her weekends at an animal **clinic**. Lin Meifeng
spends one day a week at an orphanage. And, Albert Ramirez is
spending a year abroad, training teachers in Cambodia. They are
among the millions of people who **volunteer** their time for good
5   causes.

At its heart, volunteering is about doing something to help others.
That can come in many **forms**. People can spend time with seniors
at a retirement home. Animal lovers can care for stray dogs. People
can also clean up beaches to improve the **environment**.

10   It's easy to start volunteering. Websites list local and overseas
opportunities. Some groups **organize** efforts **on a large scale**.
In 2008, the United Nations Volunteer program signed up 7,753
volunteers from 159 countries.

The work done by these
15   **generous** givers has a big
impact in every country. Many
needy people and groups
cannot **afford** to hire help. So,
they **count on** volunteers. For
20   example, in Singapore, yearly
volunteer work is valued at
around $600 million.

There is a worldwide army of volunteers giving their time. In the
USA, around one in four people are regular volunteers. Through
25   their experience, they learn new skills. They also make new friends
and **form ties with** their **communities**.

---

² orphanage – place where children without parents live
⁷ seniors – old people
⁸ stray dogs – homeless dogs
¹⁶ impact – effect
¹⁷ needy – needing help

Questions about the Reading   Choose the best answer.

1. (   ) What does Albert Ramirez do as a volunteer?
   - (A) He works at an animal clinic.
   - (B) He helps children at an orphanage.
   - (C) He helps teachers in another country.
   - (D) He works at a retirement home.

2. (   ) In the article, what is NOT mentioned as a way to volunteer?
   - (A) Visiting retired people
   - (B) Helping animals
   - (C) Building houses
   - (D) Cleaning up outdoors

3. (   ) How many volunteers worked for the United Nations Volunteer program in 2008?
   - (A) 159
   - (B) 600
   - (C) 2,008
   - (D) 7,753

4. (   ) What can we infer about the $600 million mentioned in the fourth paragraph?
   - (A) Singapore needs twice that amount.
   - (B) No one actually had to pay the money.
   - (C) It was funded by the United Nations.
   - (D) The amount was more than the previous year.

5. (   ) What does the word *opportunities* in line 11 mean?
   - (A) chances
   - (B) countries
   - (C) groups
   - (D) volunteers

Writing about the Article   Answer each question based on the article.

1. At its heart, what is volunteering about?

   It's about _____.

2. What information do volunteering websites contain?

   They contain _____.

3. In the USA, how many people are regular volunteers?

   In the USA, _____.

Vocabulary Building — Choose the best word to fill in each blank.

1. Martha was sick, so I took her to a(n) _____.
   (A) clinic　　(B) form　　(C) effort　　(D) opportunity

2. William is very _____. He loves to help other people.
   (A) organized　(B) affordable　(C) generous　(D) regular

3. Pollution from cars can badly damage the _____.
   (A) program　(B) impact　(C) weekend　(D) environment

4. TV commercials are just one _____ of advertising.
   (A) experience　(B) form　(C) training　(D) giver

5. I want to _____ a concert to benefit victims of the earthquake.
   (A) hire　　(B) afford　　(C) organize　　(D) care

6. Many people _____ to take part in international programs.
   (A) volunteer　(B) list　　(C) hire　　(D) afford

7. There are many volunteer opportunities in my _____.
   (A) senior　(B) scale　(C) community　(D) impact

8. I would love to buy a new car, but I can't _____ it.
   (A) spend　(B) train　(C) afford　(D) value

Phrase Building — Write the correct phrase in each blank. Remember to use the correct word form.

● count on　　● clean up　　● form ties with　　● on a large scale

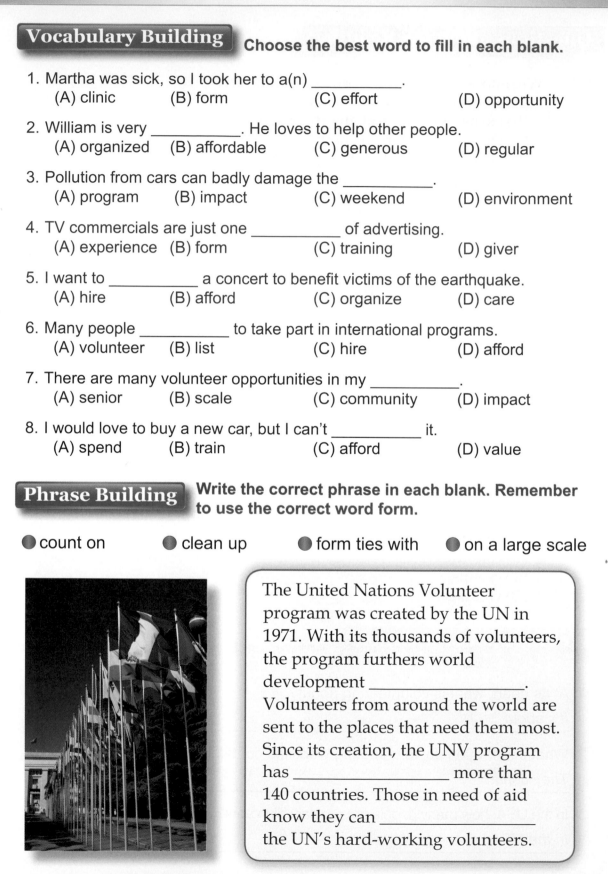

The United Nations Volunteer program was created by the UN in 1971. With its thousands of volunteers, the program furthers world development _____.
Volunteers from around the world are sent to the places that need them most. Since its creation, the UNV program has _____ more than 140 countries. Those in need of aid know they can _____ the UN's hard-working volunteers.

Grammar Exercise

Among, Through, and About

Complete each sentence with *among*, *through*, or *about*.

Example: Volunteering is _____ doing something for others.
Answer: Volunteering is *about* doing something for others.

1. _____ the rings in the case, that's the oldest.

2. _____ their hard work, they turned the restaurant into a success.

3. The story is _____ learning from your mistakes.

4. _____ good and bad times, they remained friends.

5. With its long neck, the giraffe is unique _____ land animals.

Listening Exercise Track 2

Listen to the conversation. Then, answer the following questions.

1. (   ) When will Pet Day take place?
  (A) Thursday
  (B) Friday
  (C) Saturday
  (D) Sunday

2. (   ) Why is the man unsure of attending the event?
  (A) He doesn't like to volunteer.
  (B) He isn't sure how he can help.
  (C) He thinks he will be busy.
  (D) He doesn't have any pets.

3. (   ) What is the purpose of the Pet Day event?
  (A) To feed homeless pets
  (B) To entertain pets in pet stores
  (C) To treat sick animals
  (D) To find homes for animals

Listening Activity 🔘 Track 3

Listen to the announcement. Then, fill in the information in the chart.

1. When was the food drive held?	
2. How many cans were collected?	
3. How many cans did they originally hope to collect?	
4. How many volunteers came to the event?	
5. When will the next food drive be held?	

Discussion Questions

1. In your country, where are volunteers needed the most?

2. Some programs, like the Peace Corps, require a year or more of a person's time. How would you like to volunteer for such a long time?

3. Should more people volunteer, or should the government do more to solve a country's problems? (Or should there be more of both?)

Discussion Activity

Organize a volunteer event. First, choose a cause that you would like to support. For example, do you want to help animals? How about older people? Next, decide what the event will be and what you will do to make it succeed. For example, how will you find volunteers?

Example: We are going to organize an event to plant trees on campus. We'll put up posters around school to find people to help us....

Pre-Reading Questions
Discuss these questions in pairs.

1. How much time do you spend online every day?

2. Do you belong to any Internet forums?

3. Do you spend more time with friends online or in person?

Consider the Topic
Read each statement. Check if you agree or disagree with it.

	agree	disagree
1. I met some of my best friends on the Internet.	☐	☐
2. Keeping a blog sounds like fun.	☐	☐
3. It's safe to post photos and information about yourself online.	☐	☐

Reading Passage 🔘 Track 4

1   At its heart, the Internet is about communication. Most people use the Net to meet new friends and **stay in touch** with old ones. Over the years, whole new communities have grown online. For millions of people, belonging to an Internet community is very important to
5   their lives.

Since the Internet's early years, many websites have **included** forums. People join forums to **discuss hobbies** and subjects which interest them. Besides posting public **messages**, **members** can **contact** friends through PMs (**private** messages).

10   In the mid-2000s, "social networking" sites like MySpace and Facebook grew very quickly. On these sites, members each have a page to introduce themselves
15   and blog about their lives. Photos, music, and videos can be added. And, people can leave comments on their friends' pages.

These sites are very popular. MySpace has more than 100 million
20   members. Many people spend several hours a day on the site. Updating a blog and **keeping up with** friends' pages takes a lot of time!

That worries some people. Is it **healthy** to spend so much time online? There are also questions about safety. What kinds of details
25   should people post about their lives? These are not easy questions, and we're still **figuring out** the answers.

---

[1] communication – speaking with and writing to people
[3] community – group of people who spend a lot of time together
[11] networking – bringing people together and making new friends
[21] update – add new information

Questions about the Reading Choose the best answer.

1. (   ) According to the article, what is key to the Internet?
    (A) Allowing people to contact one another
    (B) Making it easy to buy whatever you want
    (C) Reading the latest news right after it happens
    (D) Learning about new hobbies and subjects

2. (   ) What does the article suggest about Internet forums?
    (A) They have only just become popular over the last year.
    (B) They are a part of very few websites.
    (C) They include public and private ways to communicate.
    (D) They are usually visited by people at work.

3. (   ) What is NOT something people can do on Facebook?
    (A) Look for jobs
    (B) Write about daily activities
    (C) Upload personal photos
    (D) Add songs to a page

4. (   ) Why are some people worried about MySpace?
    (A) The site owners make people post personal details.
    (B) It is more popular than Facebook.
    (C) Members sometimes spend a lot of time on the site.
    (D) Not enough people have joined up.

5. (   ) What does the phrase *belonging to* in line 4 mean?
    (A) owning something
    (B) being part of
    (C) making sure of
    (D) finding out about

Writing about the Article Answer each question based on the article.

1. What do people discuss on forums?
   People write about   .

2. On social networking sites, what can people do on friends' pages?
   People can leave   .

3. How many members does MySpace have?
   The website has   .

Vocabulary Building — Choose the best word to fill in each blank.

1. That's a(n) _____ letter. I doubt your sister wants you to read it.
   (A) healthy   (B) popular   (C) easy   (D) private

2. Once a month, _____ of the movie club see a movie together.
   (A) comments   (B) members   (C) blogs   (D) subjects

3. If you have free time, I'd like to _____ an important matter with you.
   (A) discuss   (B) introduce   (C) spend   (D) add

4. Building model planes is my oldest _____. I built my first one 10 years ago.
   (A) detail   (B) answer   (C) hobby   (D) heart

5. Jack wasn't at the office, so I left a _____ with one of his colleagues.
   (A) message   (B) forum   (C) subject   (D) site

6. Does the set meal _____ a dessert?
   (A) belong   (B) leave   (C) join   (D) include

7. Are you sure it's _____ to live next to a highway? There's so much air pollution.
   (A) old   (B) early   (C) public   (D) healthy

8. If you need to _____ me, call me on my cell phone.
   (A) interest   (B) contact   (C) post   (D) worry

Phrase Building — Write the correct phrase in each blank.

● keep up with   ● stay in touch   ● figure out   ● belong to

This summer, I'll stay at my uncle's house in the countryside. I'm used to going online every day, but he doesn't have a computer. How am I going to _____ with my friends? We only chat online, so calling them on the phone won't work. Plus, I'm not sure how I'll _____ all the sports news. I guess I can watch the TV news or read the newspaper. Well, I need to _____ something soon, since I'm leaving next week!

Grammar Exercise

Adjective Clauses

Fill in each blank with *who, which,* **or** *where.*

Example: It's the town _____ I grew up.
Answer: It's the town *where* I grew up.

1. Barry is my friend _____ works at IBM.

2. This is the key _____ opens the front door.

3. Is that the building _____ you live?

4. Here are several books _____ you should read.

5. People _____ exercise a lot are usually healthy.

Listening Exercise   Track 5

Listen to the conversation. Then, answer the following questions.

1. (   ) How does the woman feel about MySpace?
    (A) It's a little confusing.
    (B) It's not hard to use.
    (C) It's a very limited service.
    (D) It's only for young people.

2. (   ) Why doesn't the man have a MySpace account?
    (A) He is not skilled at using computers.
    (B) All of the instructions are in English.
    (C) The woman won't teach him how.
    (D) His digital camera is broken.

3. (   ) What is the man interested in doing?
    (A) Keeping a blog
    (B) Chatting with friends
    (C) Sending messages
    (D) Sharing photos

11

Listening Activity 🔘 Track 6

Listen to the man. Then, fill in the information in the chart.

1. What kind of account did Rebecca get?	
2. How many friends does she want?	
3. What did Rebecca ask her brother to do?	
4. What does the man do on Wednesdays?	
5. What does the man like to do on weekends?	

Discussion Questions

1. How do you spend your time online? Do you read a lot of forums or blogs? Do you send and receive a lot of e-mails? What else?

2. Most people on sites like MySpace and Facebook are 30 years old or younger. In your opinion, why do so few older people participate?

3. Have you ever met any "Internet friends" in real life? What was the experience like?

Discussion Activity

Many people worry about criminals on social networking sites, forums, and chatrooms. It's sometimes hard to know who you can trust. Make a list of "Do's and Don'ts" for people to follow.

Example: I think it's all right to post photos of yourself. Just don't write down your full name. Posting about your hobbies and interests is also fine. But don't tell people where you work....

1. Do you own any console machines (like a Sony PlayStation)?

2. Do you like to play video games? If so, what kinds?

3. Have you ever played a game online?

Consider the Topic Read each statement. Check if you agree or disagree with it.

	agree	disagree
1. Video games are a lot of fun.	☐	☐
2. Many of my friends like playing video games.	☐	☐
3. I would like to attend a video game party.	☐	☐

Reading Passage ⊙ Track 7

1   Video games aren't just for children **anymore**. The $30 billion **industry** now **attracts** people of all ages. At the center of the industry are console machines. They can be found in millions of living rooms around the world.

5   In the past, console machines from companies like Atari and Sega were very **simple**. They could only play games. Today's machines are **along the lines of** home **entertainment** centers. Besides playing games, you can use them to look at photos, watch movies, and surf the Internet.

10   There are now three main companies making console machines: Sony, Microsoft, and Nintendo. Sony's PS3 and Microsoft's XBOX 360 **focus on** power and graphics. Serious video game players love the fast action and the look of the games. They also enjoy playing against other gamers **online**.

15   Nintendo's Wii focuses on fun and easy-to-play games. It also has a special controller. To play many games, you wave it around. For example, with Wii Tennis, you **swing**
20   the controller like a tennis racket. Many people hold "Wii parties" at their homes, with friends **coming over** to play games together.

Millions of each of these systems have
25   been sold. Over time, they'll surely bring us more **exciting** games and interesting features.

¹ billion – 1,000,000,000
⁹ surf the Internet – visit different websites
¹² graphics – images; pictures
²⁷ feature – something special that attracts people

Questions about the Reading

Choose the best answer.

1. (   ) What is the main idea?
    (A) Sega used to make simple video game machines.
    (B) Future console machines will be very powerful.
    (C) Video games now reach a very wide market.
    (D) Children love playing games in their free time.

2. (   ) What were early console machines (such as Atari) like?
    (A) They acted as home entertainment centers.
    (B) They did a great job with online gaming.
    (C) They cost much more than today's machines.
    (D) They were very limited in their features.

3. (   ) How is the Wii different from other modern gaming systems?
    (A) The system has a stronger focus on graphics.
    (B) Gamers feel it is the most powerful system.
    (C) Its games are not as difficult to learn to play.
    (D) It is the only system with sports games.

4. (   ) What is NOT a feature of today's console machines?
    (A) Going online to visit different sites
    (B) Working on school and office tasks
    (C) Playing against others on the Net
    (D) Using the machine to view photos

5. (   ) What does the word *serious* in line 12 mean?
    (A) passionate
    (B) honest
    (C) unsmiling
    (D) important

Writing about the Article

Answer each question based on the article.

1. How much is the video game industry worth?

    The industry is _____ .

2. Who are the major console machine makers?

    The three major _____ .

3. What do people do at Wii parties?

    At Wii parties, _____ .

15

Vocabulary Building

Choose the best word to fill in each blank.

1. I need to go _____ so I can check my e-mail.
   (A) Internet (B) feature (C) online (D) company

2. I'm sorry, we don't serve that kind of ice cream. We used to, but we don't _____.
   (A) all (B) anymore (C) besides (D) other

3. What a(n) _____ movie! Watching it felt just like flying through the air!
   (A) simple (B) exciting (C) serious (D) main

4. Don't _____ the bat in the house. You might break something.
   (A) play (B) find (C) swing (D) watch

5. It's a cheap Internet café, so it _____ a lot of students.
   (A) attracts (B) enjoys (C) makes (D) waves

6. Learning another language isn't so _____. It takes time and hard work.
   (A) main (B) powerful (C) sold (D) simple

7. With movies, the Internet, video games, and more, people have plenty of _____ choices.
   (A) system (B) center (C) company (D) entertainment

8. The hotel _____ is very big in this city. We have more than 200 hotels.
   (A) feature (B) player (C) past (D) industry

Phrase Building

Write the correct phrase in each blank. (Remember to use the correct word form.)

● along the lines of ● focus on ● come over ● around the world

Next month I'm having a party at my house. I'm thinking of something _____ a costume party. Or I might make it a casual dinner party. The next thing I need to _____ is a guest list. Of course I'll invite all my close friends and colleagues. I just need to make sure they don't bring too many of their own guests. At my last party, I only invited 20 people. Can you believe it? More than 50 people _____!

Grammar Exercise

Gerunds vs. Infinitives

Complete each sentence with the correct choice.

Example: I need (to call/calling) my father in a few minutes.
Answer: I need (to call)/calling) my father in a few minutes.

1. Do you enjoy (to play/playing) any sports?

2. We want (to see/seeing) the waterfall before we leave.

3. Our class plans (to visit/visiting) a museum next week.

4. She is afraid of (to leave/leaving) her house at night.

5. One of my hobbies is (to collect/collecting) buttons.

Listening Exercise Track 8

Listen to the conversation. Then, answer the following questions.

1. (   ) What did the man do yesterday?
   (A) He went running.
   (B) He called the woman.
   (C) He held a party.
   (D) He played video games.

2. (   ) What does the woman suggest?
   (A) Her friend is not very healthy.
   (B) The weather will get better soon.
   (C) It is tiring to jog every day.
   (D) She has played the Wii before.

3. (   ) What is the man considering?
   (A) Hosting a few friends this weekend
   (B) Going over to the woman's house
   (C) Attending a big event on Saturday
   (D) Buying a few new video games

Listening Activity ◎ Track 9

Listen to the report. Then, fill in the information in the chart.

1. Where is the person?	
2. How many people are there?	
3. Who has a very big booth?	
4. How much do three Nintendo games cost?	
5. How much longer will the show last?	

Discussion Questions

1. Should parents limit the amount of time their children spend playing video games? Why or why not?

2. Are video games too violent? Does playing violent video games make people behave more violently?

3. Do women and men like the same kinds of video games? What differences, if any, do you see?

Discussion Activity

Plan a Wii party with several classmates. Discuss where the party will be held, how many people you will invite, and what food you will have. Then, make a list of the kinds of games you would like to play.

Example: Our group would like a big party with around 15 people. Each of us will invite three or four other friends. The party will be at Marty's house. We'll have popcorn and potato chips....

Pre-Reading Questions

Discuss these questions in pairs.

1. Look at the picture. What do you think the man is doing?

2. How would you like to work at home several days a month?

3. How do you think companies feel about people working at home?

Consider the Topic

Read each statement. Check if you agree or disagree with it.

	agree	disagree
1. Rush hour traffic is a major problem in my city.	☐	☐
2. Very few types of office work could be done at a home office.	☐	☐
3. People who work at home usually become lazy.	☐	☐

1　In a **traditional** company, workers spend five days a week at the office. They often spend 30 minutes or longer traveling to and from work. During rush hour, traffic and **pollution** are often quite serious. Teleworking (also called "telecommuting") is one way to
5　**reduce** these problems.

Teleworkers have office jobs, but they work at home one or more days each month. Using telephones and computers with
10　Internet access, they can do all of their **regular** office tasks. Many jobs, **such as** sales, design, and even office managing, can be done at home.

15　Teleworking has many **benefits**. With fewer cars on the road, traffic and air **quality improve**. Companies save money by spending less on office space. Also, **employees** who telework are happier with their jobs.

However, some companies are slow to accept teleworking. They
20　think employees need managers **looking over their shoulder**, or they won't work hard. In fact, studies show that to be **far from the truth**. People actually get 25% more work done when they telework.

There are already more than 20 million teleworkers in Europe and
25　the USA. Japan has more than 10 million, and Australia has about 3 million. These numbers are growing, as more people learn the benefits of this 21st century working style.

---

³ rush hour – time when traffic is heaviest
¹⁰ access – chance (or way) to use something
¹¹ task – job; something you have to do
²⁷ century – period of 100 years

Questions about the Reading

Choose the best answer.

1. (   ) What does the article suggest about traditional companies?
    (A) They have many teleworkers.
    (B) Their employees spend a lot of time in traffic.
    (C) People work at the office Monday through Sunday.
    (D) Some don't have Internet access.

2. (   ) What do people need to telework?
    (A) A type of equipment that few people have
    (B) A background in sales or management
    (C) A lot of free time to work on the weekend
    (D) A phone and a way to go online

3. (   ) What are some companies worried about?
    (A) Workers getting less done away from the office
    (B) Employees spending 25% of their time at home
    (C) Studies showing that teleworking wastes time
    (D) Managers wanting to telework every day

4. (   ) About how many teleworkers does Australia have?
    (A) 3 million
    (B) 10 million
    (C) 20 million
    (D) 25 million

5. (   ) What is NOT a benefit of teleworking?
    (A) Fewer employees taking vacations
    (B) Cost savings for companies
    (C) Less pollution leading to cleaner air
    (D) Increased worker happiness

Writing about the Article

Answer each question based on the article.

1. What is common during rush hour?
   Heavy traffic and _____.

2. What jobs are suitable for teleworking?
   A lot of jobs, like _____.

3. Will the number of teleworkers probably increase or decrease?
   According to the article, _____.

21

Vocabulary Building   Choose the best word to fill in each blank.

1. With fewer cars on the road, there would be much less air _____.
   (A) style   (B) pollution   (C) traffic   (D) managing

2. Once a month, I volunteer at a clinic. For my _____ job, I work at a bank.
   (A) regular   (B) slow   (C) far   (D) long

3. Now that Paula enjoys math class, her scores are _____ every week.
   (A) saving   (B) improving   (C) accepting   (D) reducing

4. I get two weeks paid vacation every year. It's my favorite job _____.
   (A) access   (B) task   (C) manager   (D) benefit

5. This is a _____ village. People have done things the same way for 100 years.
   (A) serious   (B) long   (C) traditional   (D) hard

6. When I buy clothes, I go for top _____. I want them to last for years.
   (A) space   (B) quality   (C) sale   (D) home

7. By eating out less often, you can greatly _____ your monthly food bill.
   (A) spend   (B) learn   (C) reduce   (D) think

8. A total of 250 _____ work at the lamp factory.
   (A) offices   (B) studies   (C) employees   (D) tasks

Phrase Building   Write the correct phrase in each blank. (Remember to use the correct word form.)

⬤ in fact   ⬤ far from the truth   ⬤ such as   ⬤ look over someone's shoulder

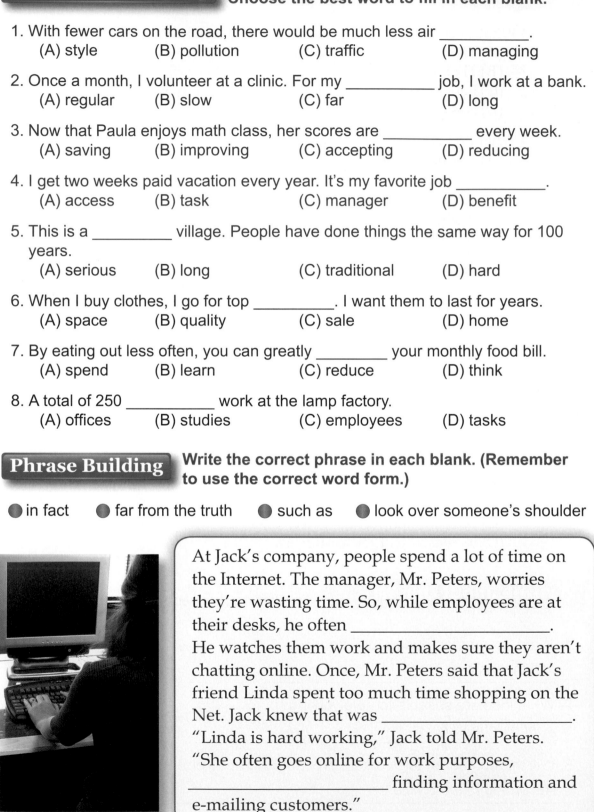

At Jack's company, people spend a lot of time on the Internet. The manager, Mr. Peters, worries they're wasting time. So, while employees are at their desks, he often _____.
He watches them work and makes sure they aren't chatting online. Once, Mr. Peters said that Jack's friend Linda spent too much time shopping on the Net. Jack knew that was _____.
"Linda is hard working," Jack told Mr. Peters. "She often goes online for work purposes, _____ finding information and e-mailing customers."

Grammar Exercise

Adverbs of Completion

Choose the correct word to complete each sentence.

Example: She isn't home (already/yet). Try calling back tonight.
Answer: She isn't home (already/yet). Try calling back tonight.

1. I'm afraid Naoki doesn't work here (still/anymore).

2. Do you (yet/still) live in Chicago?

3. I (already/anymore) sent them my job application.

4. We're not ready (still/yet). Give us a few more minutes.

5. They don't sell cookies (anymore/already). Order something else.

Listening Exercise   Track 11

Listen to the conversation. Then, answer the following questions.

1. (   ) How does the man know the woman is teleworking?
   (A) He received an e-mail from the woman.
   (B) He read about it in a newsletter.
   (C) He heard the news from a colleague.
   (D) He saw a notice posted at his office.

2. (   ) How long does the woman plan to try teleworking?
   (A) One week
   (B) One month
   (C) Several months
   (D) Half a year

3. (   ) Why doesn't the man want to telework?
   (A) His department doesn't have a program.
   (B) He wants to keep his home and work lives separate.
   (C) He needs to be at the office all day.
   (D) His drive to work only takes a few minutes.

Listening Activity ⊙ Track 12

Listen to the announcement. Then, fill in the information in the chart.

1. What kind of company is Rainbow Visions?	
2. What have employees asked about?	
3. How often may people telework?	
4. How can people sign up to telework?	
5. What should people list when signing up?	

Discussion Questions

1. What would you need in your house to set up a home office?

2. What are some good and bad points about working at home?

3. Many people meet friends (and even husbands and wives) at their workplaces. How might teleworking make that harder?

Discussion Activity

Hold a mini debate between four people in a company. On one side are two people who support letting employees telework once a week. On the other side are two people against teleworking. Divide into groups and decide which side each classmate will be on. Spend a few minutes writing down the reasons for your point of view. Then hold the mini debate.

Example: We are against teleworking. Customers often come to our office. If an employee is at home, how can he meet with them?

Pre-Reading Questions   Discuss these questions in pairs.

1. Is there a lot of graffiti where you live?

2. Does your city quickly paint over graffiti, or is it left alone?

3. In your opinion, should we treat graffiti writing as a serious crime?

Consider the Topic   Read each statement. Check if you agree or disagree with it.

	agree	disagree
1. It takes a lot of skill to make graffiti.	☐	☐
2. Graffiti makes cities more beautiful.	☐	☐
3. Cities should have areas where anybody can put graffiti up.	☐	☐

Reading Passage Track 13

1   Graffiti is a kind of street **art**. In many cities, it is seen on walls, trains, and other public places. A lot of graffiti is **illegal**, and some cities **treat** it as a serious crime. At the same time, some people see it as an important art form.

5   Graffiti became popular in the 1970s. In New York City, graffiti artists (or "writers") like Taki 183 wrote their names **all over** the city. Subway trains were popular spots.

Over the years, writers developed **creative** new **styles**. One well-known type, "bubble writing," has letters that look like large
10   bubbles. Another type is "wildstyle." The letters go in many **directions**. They often have arrows coming out of them.

Most writers choose short names, or "tags." Some **famous** ones are Seen, Ewok, and Kaws. A simple one-color tag, called a "throwup," may take just a few minutes to **paint**. More colorful
15   works of graffiti, called "pieces," can take hours or days to finish.

Illegal graffiti often has a short life. City workers might repaint the wall after a day or two. So,
20   artists take photos of their work. They send them to magazines and websites. On "legal walls," writers can freely create graffiti.
25   They don't have to **worry about** breaking the law.

³ crime – something that is against the law
⁸ develop – change and improve over time

Questions about the Reading

Choose the best answer.

1. (　) Who was Taki 183?
   (A) A New York City police officer
   (B) A subway train driver
   (C) A graffiti writer
   (D) A magazine reporter

2. (　) What is a "tag"?
   (A) A style using arrows and bubbles
   (B) A name used by a graffiti artist
   (C) A writer with a lot of experience
   (D) A work of art in a museum

3. (　) What is NOT a common place to see graffiti?
   (A) A private car
   (B) A "legal wall"
   (C) A subway train
   (D) A city wall

4. (　) What does the article suggest about "legal walls"?
   (A) They are not repainted by the city after a few days.
   (B) Magazines don't usually pay attention to them.
   (C) Writers are given free paint to write on them.
   (D) People who paint on them are breaking the law.

5. (　) According to the article, how do magazines get photographs of graffiti?
   (A) City workers give them to magazines.
   (B) Artists tell magazines where to take photos.
   (C) They receive them from graffiti writers.
   (D) Some websites let them use their photos.

Writing about the Article

Answer each question based on the article.

1. When did graffiti become popular?

   It became popular _____ .

2. What is special about wildstyle graffiti?

   The letters in wildstyle _____ .

3. How long might it take to put up a graffiti "piece"?

   It might take _____ .

Vocabulary Building

Choose the best word to fill in each blank.

1. Have you seen my dog? Which _____ did he go in?
   (A) type (B) direction (C) arrow (D) form

2. Kyoto is a _____ city in Japan. Many visitors like to go there.
   (A) legal (B) serious (C) famous (D) short

3. Today in art class, we _____ plants and flowers.
   (A) looked (B) developed (C) painted (D) wrote

4. I like this singer's _____. She has a very special voice.
   (A) style (B) worker (C) graffiti (D) spot

5. Parking here is _____. Let's find another place before we get a ticket.
   (A) public (B) popular (C) important (D) illegal

6. I like looking at _____ in museums. But I'm too poor to collect any myself.
   (A) websites (B) crime (C) art (D) magazines

7. Ms. Henderson _____ everybody well. She has a lot of friends.
   (A) chooses (B) becomes (C) creates (D) treats

8. Your daughter is very _____. She must have a good imagination.
   (A) creative (B) public (C) simple (D) large

Phrase Building

Write the correct phrase in each blank.

● over the years   ● all over   ● come out of   ● worry about

I've known Li-fen for many years. I completely trust her. _____, I've told her about all my problems and secrets. She often gives me good advice. Li-fen and I love to see new places. We've traveled _____ Asia together. Last year, we went to Thailand, and we plan to travel to Vietnam this year. Sometimes I _____ her. She's under a lot of pressure to do well at school. When she needs someone to talk to, I'm always there for her.

Grammar Exercise

Prepositions

Fill in each blank with *on*, *to*, **or** *of*.

Example: This is a good picture _____ my best friend.
Answer: This is a good picture *of* my best friend.

1. Should we hang the painting _____ this wall or that one?

2. I really like this kind _____ art.

3. Please give this package _____ your brother.

4. Is he part _____ your team?

5. There's a lot of graffiti _____ that wall.

Listening Exercise   Track 14

Listen to the conversation. Then, answer the following questions.

1. ( ) Where are the people?
    (A) At a museum
    (B) Inside a store
    (C) On a city street
    (D) In a gallery

2. ( ) What does the man say about the graffiti writer?
    (A) The writer is breaking the law.
    (B) The writer is young.
    (C) The writer is a troublemaker.
    (D) The writer is skillful.

3. ( ) What do the people disagree about?
    (A) Whether graffiti is everywhere
    (B) Whether the graffiti is well done
    (C) Whether other people like graffiti
    (D) Whether the graffiti should be there

Listening Activity 🔘 Track 15

Listen to the report. Then, fill in the information in the chart.

1. When was the contest held?	
2. Where was the contest held?	
3. What were the walls made of?	
4. How long did artists have to work?	
5. Who chose the winner?	

Discussion Questions

1. What areas in your city have the most graffiti?

2. In your city, should graffiti be allowed on some buildings or walls? Or should it be illegal everywhere?

3. In your opinion, why do so many young people want to put up graffiti? Why not just draw or paint something on paper?

Discussion Activity

Working in groups of three or four classmates, form two sides (with one or two students on each side). One side supports artists who make graffiti. The other sees graffiti as a serious problem. Each side gives its reasons for its point of view. Then, try to find a solution that will make both sides happy.

Example: We support graffiti artists. A lot of our city walls are really ugly. We think that street art makes them more beautiful....

Cell Phone Novels 6

Pre-Reading Questions Discuss these questions in pairs.

1. What kinds of books do you like to read?

2. Do you often receive cell phone text messages?

3. How would you like to read a story on your cell phone?

Consider the Topic Read each statement. Check if you agree or disagree with it.

	agree	disagree
1. I carry my cell phone everywhere I go.	☐	☐
2. Cell phone screens are hard to read.	☐	☐
3. These days, people don't read enough books.	☐	☐

Reading Passage 🔘 Track 16

1   In the 19th century, newspapers often **published novels** in parts. Chapters were printed **one at a time**. Telling the whole story took several weeks or months. At the start of the 21st century, the cell phone novel was born. It married an old idea with new
5   **technology**.

There are several ways to read a cell phone novel. Readers may go to special **websites** to read a chapter or download it to their phone. Or, chapters may be sent to a person's phone via e-mail or short message. Chapters are short – often **no more than** a few hundred
10   words long.

The first cell phone novel, *Deep Love*, was written by Yoshi, a Japanese writer. It was very popular. In fact, the story was later published as a book and made into a movie. Other Japanese authors, like Naito and Chaco, have also been **successful** in the
15   field.

The first Chinese cell phone novel was *Distance*. It was written in 2004 by Taiwanese writer Xuan Huang. The story **contained** 1008 characters and was **divided** into 15 chapters.

20   There are also cell phone novels in French, English, and other languages. Romance and horror stories are very popular. Thousands of these mini novels are **on the market**. It's a fast, easy, and **convenient** way to read a great story.

---

2 chapter – section of a book
14 author – writer
18 character – Chinese word
21 horror story – story that makes you scared

Questions about the Reading   Choose the best answer.

1. (   ) When did cell phone novels become popular?
    (A) In the late 18th century
    (B) In the 19th century
    (C) In the middle of the 20th century
    (D) In the early 21st century

2. (   ) What do cell phone novels and novels in newspapers have in common?
    (A) They are both products of modern technology.
    (B) They are both told in parts.
    (C) They are both, on average, a few hundred words long.
    (D) They are both printed on paper.

3. (   ) Which of the following is NOT true about *Deep Love*?
    (A) Naito was the writer.
    (B) Many people liked it.
    (C) It was made into a movie.
    (D) Its author was Japanese.

4. (   ) Who is Xuan Huang?
    (A) The world's first cell phone novelist
    (B) A reporter for a Chinese newspaper
    (C) A person who has written 15 novels
    (D) The writer of the novel *Distance*

5. (   ) What is suggested about cell phone novels?
    (A) Horror stories are read by many fans.
    (B) Less than 1,000 are on the market.
    (C) Most of them are written in English.
    (D) Expensive phones are needed to read them.

Writing about the Article   Answer each question based on the article.

1. Who wrote the first cell phone novel?

    The first cell phone novel was _____ .

2. How many characters did *Distance* have?

    Distance had _____ .

3. What languages have cell phone novels been written in?

    They have been written _____ .

Vocabulary Building — Choose the best word to fill in each blank.

1. There's a lot of work to do. I'll _____ it into small jobs for each of you.
   (A) write   (B) send   (C) make   (D) divide

2. I take a lot of photos. I want to find a(n) _____ where I can post them to share with friends.
   (A) phone   (B) website   (C) idea   (D) story

3. Our house is in a(n) _____ area. There are many stores nearby.
   (A) easy   (B) whole   (C) convenient   (D) fast

4. It's hard to read a(n) _____ in another language.
   (A) field   (B) novel   (C) century   (D) movie

5. Was the book _____ recently? If so, it will be in the New Products section.
   (A) published   (B) read   (C) told   (D) born

6. Computers used to take up a whole room. With today's _____, they can fit in your hand.
   (A) chapter   (B) language   (C) message   (D) technology

7. The store was so _____, they soon opened a second branch.
   (A) whole   (B) new   (C) successful   (D) short

8. How many bottles does the box _____?
   (A) contain   (B) download   (C) publish   (D) divide

Phrase Building — Write the correct phrase in each blank.

● no more than   ● on the market   ● at the start   ● one at a time

Later this year, T-Shirt World will release a series of limited-edition t-shirts. The first design will be _____ on July 15th. Only 50 pieces will be sold, and people can only buy them at T-Shirt World's main store in San Francisco. Other designs in the series will be released _____, with the second design going on sale on August 1st. There will be a total of seven new designs. _____ 100 pieces of each style will be sold.

Grammar Exercise

The Passive Voice

Write the correct form of the word(s) in parentheses.

Example: The house was (build) _____ several years ago.
Answer: The house was *built* several years ago.

1. The money was (steal) _____ by the thief.

2. Many trees were (knock down) _____ during the storm.

3. Do you know how these dolls are (make) _____?

4. All the hotel rooms are (clean) _____ in the afternoon.

5. When was the company (found) _____?

Listening Exercise Track 17

Listen to the conversation. Then, answer the following questions.

1. (   ) What does the man ask the woman about?
   (A) The length of a new cell phone novel
   (B) The title of a popular mystery story
   (C) The news about a killer in the city
   (D) The situation with a novel's chapter

2. (   ) How many chapters are in *Supermarket Killers*?
   (A) 5
   (B) 16
   (C) 20
   (D) 30

3. (   ) What does the man hope will happen?
   (A) The novel's author will write longer stories.
   (B) The price of cell phone novels will go down.
   (C) The woman will tell him about the ending.
   (D) The killer will be caught by the police.

Listening Activity 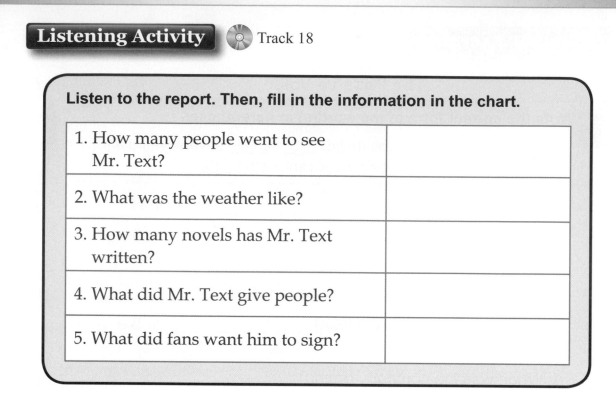 Track 18

Listen to the report. Then, fill in the information in the chart.

1. How many people went to see Mr. Text?	
2. What was the weather like?	
3. How many novels has Mr. Text written?	
4. What did Mr. Text give people?	
5. What did fans want him to sign?	

Discussion Questions

1. Besides making phone calls, what do you often use your cell phone for?

2. Cell phone novels are usually much shorter than printed novels. What's good and bad about reading very short stories?

3. Will the day come when everything we read is on a screen? That is, will people completely stop reading things printed on paper?

Discussion Activity

Working with several classmates, plan your own cell phone novel. What kind of story will it be? How many words will each chapter have? How many total chapters will it have? If possible, write the first 50 words of the first chapter.

Example: Our novel is a romance. It's about two people living on an island. Each chapter will be 200 words long, so people can read a chapter very quickly....

Pre-Reading Questions
Discuss these questions in pairs

1. What is your favorite place to shop?

2. Do you ever shop at small boutiques?

3. What goods from overseas do people in your country like? (clothes? jewelry?)

Consider the Topic
Read each statement. Check if you agree or disagree with it.

	agree	disagree
1. I try to follow overseas fashion trends.	☐	☐
2. I like shopping at small shops more than at department stores.	☐	☐
3. The Internet makes it easier to buy what I want.	☐	☐

Reading Passage 🔘 Track 19

1 In the past, people looking for imported goods usually shopped at department stores. Nowadays, shopping 5 at small boutiques is very popular. Often, these stores only have one person (the **owner**) working there. They **offer fashionable** new 10 products and great **service**.

Boutiques can be found in every large city in Taiwan. In Taipei, there are many in Ximending and eastern Taipei. In Taichung, the Fengchia night market is a great area. And in Kaohsiung, the Shinkuchan area has many boutiques.

15 To buy new **stock**, the boss may travel to Japan, Korea, or elsewhere. Then, he or she brings everything back to Taiwan to sell. Or, the owner may have a friend in another country who can **lend a hand** with buying the goods.

Boutiques sell a **range** of fashionable products. Shirts, hats, and 20 shoes are popular. So are jewelry, makeup, and bags. Shop owners also take special orders from customers.

The Internet is important to this type of business. It makes it easy for people to **get in touch with** each other, **view** photos of 25 the latest goods, and place orders. **Above all**, small shop owners work very hard. Thanks to them, what's fashionable in Tokyo today may be seen in Taipei next week, or **even** sooner!

---

2 imported – brought in from another country
5 boutique – small store
25 latest – newest

Questions about the Reading   Choose the best answer.

1. (   ) What is the main idea?
   (A) Department stores are less popular than they once were.
   (B) Boutiques help people get new products from overseas.
   (C) Small stores are the cheapest places to get Japanese clothes.
   (D) Everybody likes to have fashionable clothes and bags.

2. (   ) According to the article, what is one way boutiques get new goods?
   (A) From friends in other countries
   (B) From clothing catalogues
   (C) From large department stores
   (D) From sellers in Taiwan

3. (   ) Where can people find many boutiques in Kaohsiung?
   (A) The Ximending area
   (B) The Fengchia night market
   (C) The Shinkuchan area
   (D) The Love River area

4. (   ) What is NOT mentioned as something you can get at a boutique?
   (A) Jewelry
   (B) Hats
   (C) Bags
   (D) Cameras

5. (   ) How does the Internet help boutiques?
   (A) It lets everyone see photos right away.
   (B) It makes it easier to get discounts.
   (C) It is the only safe way to order new goods.
   (D) It does everything, so shop owners don't work hard.

Writing about the Article   Answer each question based on the article.

1. Oftentimes, how many people work at a boutique?

   Often, only _____ .

2. What do shop owners do after buying goods in other countries?

   After shopping overseas, they _____ .

3. What can a customer do if a shop doesn't have what he or she wants?

   In that case, the customer can _____ .

Vocabulary Building   Choose the best word to fill in each blank.

1. We sell clothes from around the world, but most of our _____ comes from Europe.
   (A) shop   (B) goods   (C) Internet   (D) stock

2. I can _____ you $30 for the necklace. Do we have a deal?
   (A) offer   (B) sell   (C) shop   (D) buy

3. Meals for two people at the restaurant are in the $60-$80 _____.
   (A) product   (B) range   (C) customer   (D) order

4. Your clothes are all so _____. You look like a model!
   (A) hard   (B) easy   (C) fashionable   (D) latest

5. This coffee shop has great _____. The staff is very friendly and helpful.
   (A) business   (B) boss   (C) service   (D) everything

6. Who is the _____ of the black car parked outside? You need to move it immediately.
   (A) order   (B) owner   (C) area   (D) choice

7. This printer is great. It lets you _____ each photo before you print it.
   (A) make   (B) look   (C) shop   (D) view

8. My niece is talented. She paints, writes songs, and _____ plays the violin.
   (A) even   (B) very   (C) other   (D) every

Phrase Building   Write the correct phrase in each blank. (Remember to use the correct word form.)

● lend a hand   ● get in touch with   ● above all   ● place an order

These days, I'm very busy. Besides going to university, I have a part-time job. Lucky for me, my sister goes to the same school. She's great with computers, so she _____ when I need help writing a program. I know a lot about history, so when she has a question, she _____ me. It's great that we can help each other out. _____, it's nice to have her nearby, since we get to spend a lot of time together.

Grammar Exercise

Everything, Anything, and Nothing

Fill in each blank with *everything*, *anything*, **or** *nothing*.

Example: We lost _____ during the storm. We're really in trouble.

Answer: We lost *everything* during the storm. We're really in trouble.

1. I don't have _____ left to say. I've told you what I know.

2. There's _____ left in the refrigerator. Let's go shopping.

3. Is there _____ else in the car? Let me know, and I'll bring it into the house.

4. I love _____ about this place. It's perfect.

5. _____ will change my mind. I've made my decision.

Listening Exercise   Track 20

Listen to the conversation. Then, answer the following questions.

1. (   ) Who is Toto?
   (A) The woman's friend
   (B) A small shop owner
   (C) A clothing designer
   (D) The man's brother

2. (   ) What does the man suggest about the store's service?
   (A) It's fast and friendly.
   (B) People can order anything they want.
   (C) The fee is a little high.
   (D) It covers items from very few countries.

3. (   ) What does the woman want to do?
   (A) Place an order herself
   (B) Try on the man's jacket
   (C) Take a trip to England
   (D) Help a friend buy something

Listening Activity Track 21

Listen to the description. Then, fill in the information in the chart.

1. What countries does the person buy from?	
2. How much is the basic service charge?	
3. How long will the person wait in line before charging extra?	
4. How much is the extra charge?	
5. What is the maximum item weight?	

Discussion Questions

1. Have you ever gone shopping in another city or country? What did you buy?

2. Limited-edition shirts, shoes, and jackets are often sold at boutiques. Will you try harder to get something if it is limited to just a few hundred pieces?

3. Small boutiques often have just a few items for sale. Yet these shops are popular. Why do many people prefer them over large shops?

Discussion Activity

Imagine you and several classmates are going to open your own boutique. What kinds of things will your shop sell? Where will you get your stock? Remember to name your shop!

Example: We decided to open a European style clothing shop. We'll sell jackets, pants, and other things from Europe. I have a cousin in France, so he'll help us buy stuff....

Discuss these questions in pairs.

1. Do you pay a lot of attention to news about space?

2. How would you like to visit the International Space Station?

3. What do you think traveling in space would be like? (exciting? scary?)

Consider the Topic Read each statement. Check if you agree or disagree with it.

	agree	disagree
1. I would be too afraid to take a trip into space.	☐	☐
2. If it were possible, I would like to stay at a hotel in space.	☐	☐
3. One day, space tourism will be cheap.	☐	☐

Reading Passage 🔘 Track 22

1   For the first 40 years of space flight, only professional astronauts traveled into **space**. The rest of us had to watch them on television. That is all **changing**, as private **tourists** are now taking trips high above **Earth**.

5   In 2001, Dennis Tito became the first space tourist. He paid $20 million to fly in a Russian rocket to the International Space Station. **Afterwards**, several other tourists paid a high price for the week-long **trip**.

     In 2004, SpaceShipOne became the first privately built ship to fly
10   into space. Soon afterwards, the company started building larger versions of the ship. Its first customer, Virgin Galactic, **plans** to take people more than 100 kilometers above Earth. Each trip will include four minutes spent in space. The first tickets have a price tag of about $200,000. However, Virgin says that should soon **come down**
15   to $50,000.

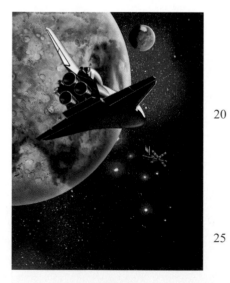

Several other companies are building ships to take people into space. Others are building space hotels. **Believe it or not**, some companies even have
20 plans for trips around the moon!

Spaceports will be the starting points for these **amazing** trips. They are being built in Singapore, the UAE, and the USA. Indeed, in a few years,
25 thousands of people may **head to** spaceports on their way into space.

¹ astronaut – person who travels in space
⁶ rocket – type of space ship
¹² kilometer – 1 kilometer equals 0.62 miles
¹² include – come with
²¹ spaceport – like an airport, but for space ships

Questions about the Reading
Choose the best answer.

1. (   ) What is the main idea?
  - (A) It's very expensive to fly to the space station.
  - (B) The first people traveled into space 40 years ago.
  - (C) Spaceports are key to the future of space travel.
  - (D) Soon, many people may take trips into space.

2. (   ) When did Mr. Tito fly to the International Space Station?
  - (A) 1968
  - (B) 2001
  - (C) 2004
  - (D) 2010

3. (   ) About how much will Virgin Galactic's first passengers pay?
  - (A) $50,000
  - (B) $100,000
  - (C) $200,000
  - (D) $20,000,000

4. (   ) What is NOT being planned for space tourists?
  - (A) A stay at a space hotel
  - (B) Four-hour space walks
  - (C) Trips around the moon
  - (D) Short flights into space

5. (   ) What does the word *version* in line 11 mean?
  - (A) story
  - (B) flight
  - (C) model
  - (D) report

Writing about the Article
Answer each question based on the article.

1. What was the name of the first private ship to travel into space?

   The name of _____ .

2. How high will people travel in Virgin Galactic's ships?

   Travelers will fly _____ .

3. What countries are building spaceports?

   Spaceports are being built _____ .

Vocabulary Building

Choose the best word to fill in each blank.

1. Let's take a _____ to Europe this year. How about France?
   (A) version   (B) tourist   (C) trip   (D) minute

2. We can't _____ the time the bus leaves. It's fixed.
   (A) watch   (B) build   (C) change   (D) pay

3. I'm just a(n) _____ in Paris. I'm going home on Friday.
   (A) ship   (B) company   (C) astronaut   (D) tourist

4. Your drawing is _____. It looks just like your mother.
   (A) private   (B) amazing   (C) high   (D) international

5. There is no air in _____. So, we have to wear special suits to breathe.
   (A) space   (B) hotel   (C) ship   (D) moon

6. It's time for me to go to the concert. _____, I'll tell you all about it.
   (A) Now   (B) Even   (C) Afterwards   (D) First

7. Elephants are the largest land animals on _____.
   (A) Earth   (B) moon   (C) rocket   (D) space

8. If we have any money left, we _____ to go out for ice cream after dinner.
   (A) travel   (B) include   (C) take   (D) plan

Phrase Building

Write the correct phrase in each blank. (Remember to use the correct word form.)

● believe it or not   ● head to   ● come down   ● on the way

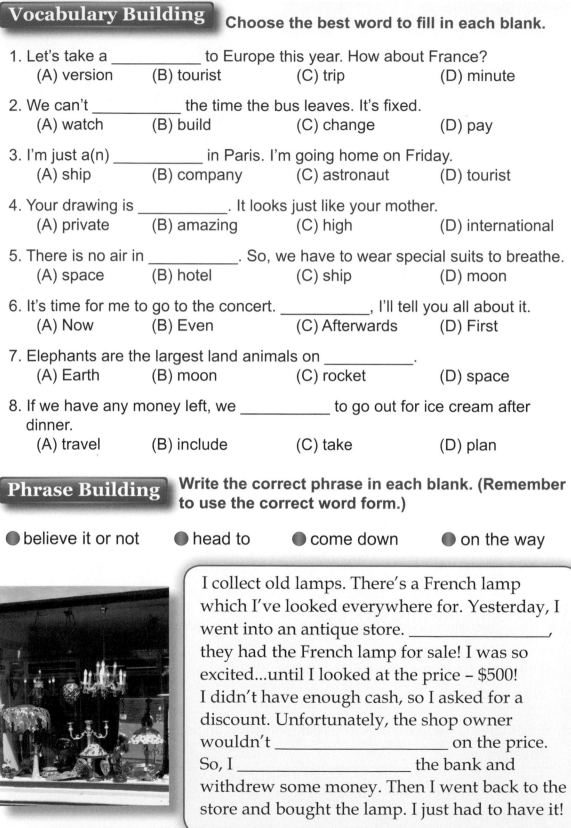

I collect old lamps. There's a French lamp which I've looked everywhere for. Yesterday, I went into an antique store. _____, they had the French lamp for sale! I was so excited...until I looked at the price – $500! I didn't have enough cash, so I asked for a discount. Unfortunately, the shop owner wouldn't _____ on the price. So, I _____ the bank and withdrew some money. Then I went back to the store and bought the lamp. I just had to have it!

Grammar Exercise

Even, Even if, and Not even

Complete each sentence with *even*, *even if*, **or** *not even*.

Example: _____ it is raining, we will hold the race.
Answer: *Even if* it is raining, we will hold the race.

1. All of my relatives came – _____ my cousin from New Zealand.

2. _____ the ring is expensive, I will buy it.

3. On farms, _____ children can ride a horse. Everybody learns to do it.

4. _____ David, who is very strong, could lift the table. So, we gave up.

5. The museum was _____ bigger than we expected.

Listening Exercise Track 23

Listen to the conversation. Then, answer the following questions.

1. ( ) How did the man get the ticket to travel into space?
    (A) He bought it from a friend.
    (B) He went onto a TV game show.
    (C) He won an Internet contest.
    (D) He received it as a prize.

2. ( ) How much will the man pay?
    (A) $10,000
    (B) $20,000
    (C) $200,000
    (D) Nothing

3. ( ) How does the man feel about the trip?
    (A) Nervous
    (B) Excited
    (C) Worried
    (D) Uncertain

Listening Activity Track 24

Listen to the report. Then, fill in the information in the chart.

1. What do Rita and Fred want to do?	
2. What do they already have?	
3. What do they need for the ceremony?	
4. How are they raising money?	
5. What will they do with the money?	

Discussion Questions

1. Imagine you could travel anywhere, including any place on Earth or even outer space. Where would you go?

2. Early space tourists spent a huge amount of money for the trip. In your opinion, why would someone spend so much for just a few days in space?

3. How would a trip into space be different from a trip to another city or country on Earth?

Discussion Activity

Design a space hotel. Decide if it will be floating in space, on the moon, or on another planet. What will the rooms be like? Will the hotel have any special features? How will guests get from Earth to your hotel? Finally, don't forget to name your hotel!

Example: The rooms in our space hotel will be round. They will have really big windows, so people can look out at the stars....

Pre-Reading Questions

Discuss these questions in pairs.

1. Do you have any friends from other countries?

2. What is a gift you would *never* give someone?

3. When eating, are there any actions that would be very rude?

Consider the Topic

Read each statement. Check if you agree or disagree with it.

	agree	disagree
1. Before going abroad, we should learn about the other country's culture.	☐	☐
2. It is rude to ask people about their salary.	☐	☐
3. Young people care more about being polite than their parents.	☐	☐

Reading Passage ⊙ Track 25

1   To understand a **foreign** country, we need to learn about its **culture**. Certainly, it's helpful to study the language and history. But it's also a good idea to learn what not to do. Things which are strongly unacceptable are called taboos.

5   Eating taboos are found throughout the world. In many Asian cultures, chopsticks should never be left standing up in a rice bowl. In India, touching food with one's left hand is **seen as** unclean. And, in Muslim cultures, people do not eat pork.

Interestingly, a taboo in one
10   country may not be a problem in another. For example, in Chinese culture, giving clocks as gifts is **frowned on**. But that would be fine in America.
15   In fact, a beautiful clock would be a thoughtful gift.

The same goes for some conversation **topics**. In many Western cultures, it's **rude** to ask about a person's age, weight, or **salary**. However, these topics may not be as **sensitive** in East Asia.

20   For sure, understanding what not to do can be hard. **Fortunately**, there are many websites about taboos. Travel guidebooks often have a section on the topic. It's **worth taking time** to understand another culture's taboos. It shows our respect for our friends around the world.

2 certainly – definitely
4 unacceptable – not allowed; not proper
8 Muslim – following the religion of Islam

Questions about the Reading
Choose the best answer.

1. (   ) What is the main idea?
   - (A) Learning about taboos helps us understand other cultures.
   - (B) People should try hard to be polite to foreign visitors.
   - (C) Some cultures have more taboos than others.
   - (D) Often, the most interesting taboos are related to eating.

2. (   ) What is suggested about eating with one's left hand?
   - (A) It is a serious taboo in Muslim cultures.
   - (B) It is thought of as a dirty action in India.
   - (C) It is done in cultures throughout the world.
   - (D) It is only a taboo in one Asian culture.

3. (   ) According to the article, which of the following is true?
   - (A) It is polite to give someone a clock in Korea.
   - (B) Asking about someone's weight is rude everywhere.
   - (C) People in America don't like talking about their age.
   - (D) Most countries have one or more taboos in common.

4. (   ) What does the word *thoughtful* in line 16 mean?
   - (A) meaningful
   - (B) serious
   - (C) expensive
   - (D) beautiful

5. (   ) How does the article suggest people learn more about taboos?
   - (A) By teaching foreign friends about their culture
   - (B) By going onto the Internet
   - (C) By speaking with people from other countries
   - (D) By watching television

Writing about the Article
Answer each question based on the article.

1. Besides learning about taboos, how else can people understand another country?
   People can also study _____ .

2. What type of taboo is found all over the world?
   Many countries have _____ .

3. What is something people do not do in Muslim cultures?
   In Muslim cultures, people _____ .

Vocabulary Building Choose the best word to fill in each blank.

1. Mr. Richards doesn't like talking about his job. It would be _____ to ask him about it.
   (A) thoughtful   (B) strong   (C) fine   (D) rude

2. Jenny's monthly _____ is low, so she can't afford to buy a house.
   (A) taboo   (B) salary   (C) section   (D) weight

3. It's a very rare car. It's _____ many thousands of dollars.
   (A) sure   (B) worth   (C) about   (D) called

4. Weather is a popular conversation _____.
   (A) problem   (B) gift   (C) topic   (D) fact

5. Before you go to a(n) _____ country, you need to get a passport.
   (A) foreign   (B) hard   (C) beautiful   (D) unacceptable

6. The movie is so boring! _____, it will be over soon.
   (A) Strongly   (B) Certainly   (C) Interestingly (D) Fortunately

7. Chinese _____ is very interesting, especially the holidays and customs.
   (A) culture   (B) language   (C) age   (D) respect

8. Kevin is a(n) _____ guy. Sad movies make him cry.
   (A) rude   (B) sensitive   (C) unclean   (D) same

Phrase Building Write the correct phrase in each blank. (Remember to use the correct word form.)

● seen as   ● frown on   ● learn about   ● take time

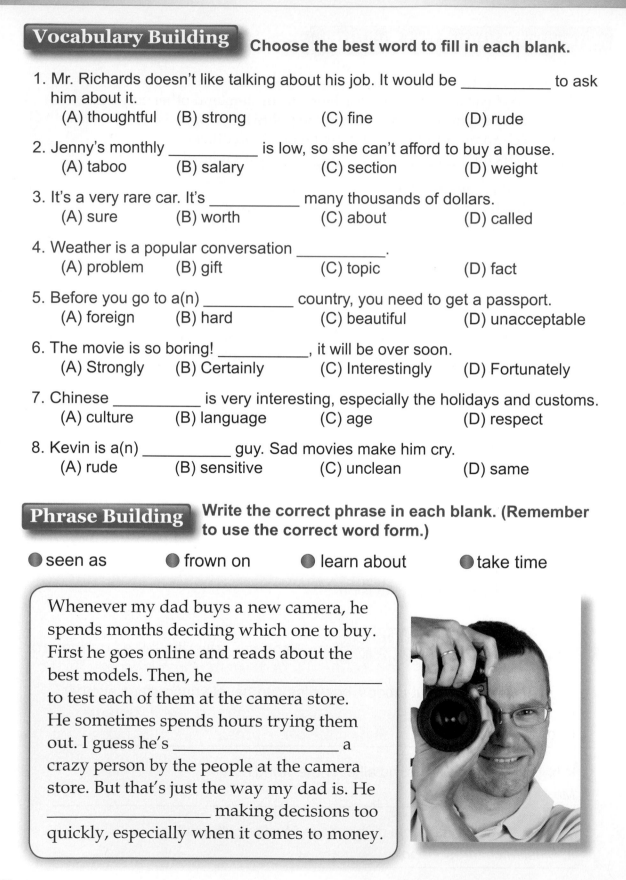

Whenever my dad buys a new camera, he spends months deciding which one to buy. First he goes online and reads about the best models. Then, he _____ to test each of them at the camera store. He sometimes spends hours trying them out. I guess he's _____ a crazy person by the people at the camera store. But that's just the way my dad is. He _____ making decisions too quickly, especially when it comes to money.

Grammar Exercise

Adjectives vs. Adverbs

Complete each sentence with the correct choice.

Example: Shawn was very (helpful/helpfully) during our visit.
Answer: Shawn was very (helpful/helpfully) during our visit.

1. Thank you very much for the (thoughtful/thoughtfully) gift.

2. He (quick/quickly) opened the package after it arrived.

3. (Fortunate/Fortunately), there's enough food for everyone.

4. I thought the picture was (beautiful/beautifully) painted.

5. Fiona was (angry/angrily) when she heard what happened.

Listening Exercise   Track 26

Listen to the conversation. Then, answer the following questions.

1. (   ) Whose birthday was it?
    (A) Zhi Ming's
    (B) Isabella's
    (C) Ichiro's
    (D) Celine's

2. (   ) What is suggested about giving people clocks?
    (A) It is a very common gift.
    (B) It is an expensive present.
    (C) It is a rude thing to do.
    (D) It is done on some holidays.

3. (   ) What did Ichiro do?
    (A) He gave something to another student.
    (B) He helped a friend understand something.
    (C) He told an Italian person to accept a gift.
    (D) He listened to someone explain a taboo.

Listening Activity ◉ Track 27

Listen to the advertisement. Then, fill in the information in the chart.

1. What is the person selling?	
2. What part of the world is the product about?	
3. Name one situation that will be shown.	
4. Name one skill that will be taught.	
5. What free gift can someone get?	

Discussion Questions

1. In your culture, are taboos more or less important than 30 years ago? Do most people still try to avoid them?

2. Imagine you see a visitor in your country committing a taboo. Will you tell the person that he or she is doing something wrong?

3. Businesspeople need to be careful not to commit taboos. What's the best way for them to avoid such problems?

Discussion Activity

Role play two people in your country having dinner with a foreign guest. (One student is the guest. The other two students are people from your country.) The foreign guest commits a serious taboo. (You decide what it is.) What happens next? How does the foreign guest react?

Example: **Student A**: Greta, can I mention something?

Student B: Sure, go ahead.

Student A: Well, in my country, people don't pick up food with their hands while eating....

Mark Chang: Toy Designer 10

Pre-Reading Questions Discuss these questions in pairs.

1. Do you collect anything? (for example, stamps, coins, etc.)

2. What kinds of art do you like?

3. Do you do any art yourself? If so, what kind?

Consider the Topic Read each statement. Check if you agree or disagree with it.

	agree	disagree
1. It would be fun to design my own toy.	☐	☐
2. I often go to galleries and museums.	☐	☐
3. I like learning about art from around the world.	☐	☐

55

Reading Passage 🎧 Track 28

1   Toys are not just for children anymore. Many students and office workers **collect** them to display on their desks. Mark Chang, from Taipei, is a **professional** artist and toy designer. His work is a **top notch** example of **modern** Taiwanese **design**.

5   Mark studied architecture at Tamkang University and computer design at Chiao Tung University. He has worked in several design **fields**, like architecture and animation. In
10 2004, Mark started Phalanx, a design company, as well as Pixie, a toy store and art gallery.

At Pixie, people can buy many interesting toys. They are designed by
15 artists from France, England, Taiwan, and other countries. **In addition**, Pixie sells toys designed by Mark.

One of Mark's toy lines is called SoWhat. The figures show Mark's excellent sense of shape and color. Mark has designed many
20 versions of the SoWhat toys. The line has a lot of fans. In fact, Jay Chou even designed a **special** version of the figure.

Mark also **enjoys** working with other artists. Phalanx has **put out** toys designed by artists from Japan, the USA, and **elsewhere**. At the same time, Phalanx sells Mark's toys to shops all over the world.
25 For sure, Mark Chang is a Taiwanese artist with an international outlook.

---

² display – show
⁵ architecture – the field of designing buildings
⁹ animation – moving images (like cartoons)
²⁶ outlook – point of view; way of looking at things

Questions about the Reading   Choose the best answer.

1. (   ) According to the article, who collects toys these days?
   (A) Mostly children and designers
   (B) Workers in every office
   (C) Collectors with large desks
   (D) Many people, including students

2. (   ) What did Mark Chang do in 2004?
   (A) He attended university.
   (B) He worked with Jay Chou.
   (C) He opened a toy store.
   (D) He traveled to France.

3. (   ) What is NOT something people can do at Pixie?
   (A) Buy toys created by Mark
   (B) Spend time with Jay Chou
   (C) Look at designs from England
   (D) Find out about SoWhat toys

4. (   ) What is suggested about SoWhat figures?
   (A) They are the only toys made by Phalanx.
   (B) The figures are all the same shape and color.
   (C) Collectors can buy them outside of Taiwan.
   (D) There are very few versions of the toys.

5. (   ) What does the word *line* in line 20 mean?
   (A) series
   (B) course
   (C) limit
   (D) stripe

Writing about the Article   Answer each question based on the article.

1. Where did Mark study computer design?

   He studied   .

2. Besides Mark, who has designed a SoWhat figure?

   A special version   .

3. Mark has worked with artists from which countries?

   He has worked with   .

Vocabulary Building
Choose the best word to fill in each blank.

1. This store doesn't sell the phone I'm looking for. Let's look _____.
   (A) over   (B) anymore   (C) elsewhere   (D) even

2. Jane is interested in advertising. She hopes to enter the _____ after finishing university.
   (A) field   (B) outlook   (C) sense   (D) design

3. My father is a(n) _____ piano player. He plays every night at a club.
   (A) interesting   (B) other   (C) international   (D) professional

4. I _____ stamps. My favorite is this one, from South Africa.
   (A) work   (B) collect   (C) start   (D) call

5. This is a _____ kind of tea. The leaves only grow high up in the mountains.
   (A) special   (B) professional   (C) modern   (D) same

6. Some people really _____ ghost stories. They love being scared.
   (A) enjoy   (B) display   (C) work   (D) show

7. I love your car's _____. It's not too big, but it easily seats six people.
   (A) line   (B) store   (C) design   (D) art

8. My school is very _____. Every desk in every classroom has a computer connected to the Internet.
   (A) elsewhere   (B) top   (C) same   (D) modern

Phrase Building
Write the correct phrase in each blank.

● for sure   ● in addition   ● top notch   ● put out

Once a week, there's an artists' market at a local park. A lot of _____ artists bring handmade goods to sell. There are several art schools in the area, so the quality is great. There are usually 10 or 20 painters. _____, several potters bring their cups, bowls, and other beautiful works. One of them, Mindy Fields, often sells out of everything. But, every week, she keeps bringing new stuff. I don't know how she has time to _____ so many pieces!

Grammar Exercise

Elsewhere, Anywhere, and Somewhere

Fill in each blank with *elsewhere, anywhere,* **or** *somewhere.*

Example: They don't have the DVD here, so we'll have to buy it
_____.

Answer: They don't have the DVD here, so we'll have to buy it
elsewhere.

1. I can't find my glasses _____. Have you seen them?

2. There are people here from Germany, Brazil, Korea, and
_____.

3. We've arrived. Now, I need to find _____ to park.

4. The cat is hiding _____ in this area. Let's find it.

5. Put your jacket _____. It doesn't matter where.

Listening Exercise   Track 29

Listen to the conversation. Then, answer the following questions.

1. (　) Why didn't the man attend the show?
   (A) He took his family on a trip.
   (B) He didn't know when it was.
   (C) He was too busy with work.
   (D) He didn't have enough money.

2. (　) What was the problem at the show?
   (A) Everything was expensive.
   (B) Many people were there.
   (C) The location was hard to find.
   (D) It was far from the man's office.

3. (　) What did the woman do at the show?
   (A) She took a lot of photos.
   (B) She met many artists.
   (C) She bought a lot of toys.
   (D) She waited in several lines.

Listening Activity ◉ Track 30

Listen to the advertisement. Then, fill in the information in the chart.

1. What kind of store is it?	
2. How do people get a mini toy?	
3. What do people exchange for the secret toy?	
4. How many mini toys were made?	
5. How many secret toys were made?	

Discussion Questions

1. What kinds of toys did you play with when you were a child?

2. In recent years, toy collecting has become very popular with adults. Why do you think that is?

3. Is it all right for adults to play with the toys they collect? Or, should they just buy them, put them on a shelf, and leave them alone?

Discussion Activity

Good news! Your company has chosen you to design a new toy! What kind of toy will you design? (a doll? a robot? a car? something else?) What features will it have? How big will it be? Is it for adults or children? If possible, take out a piece of paper and draw your toy. When you're finished, tell the rest of the class about your design.

Example: We have designed a giant monster, called Ginosaur. Ginosaur will be made of plastic. It will be two feet tall and will have six legs....

Pre-Reading Questions — Discuss these questions in pairs.

1. Do you know many people from other countries?

2. In your city, is there a special area where people from other countries get together?

3. Do you know anyone married to a person from another culture?

Consider the Topic — Read each statement. Check if you agree or disagree with it.

	agree	disagree
1. It's easy to adjust to living in a new country.	☐	☐
2. Communities with people from many different cultures are interesting.	☐	☐
3. It's fun to eat at restaurants that serve food from other countries.	☐	☐

Reading Passage Track 31

1   Over the last 200 years, worldwide immigration has quickly grown.
    That has led to many countries becoming multicultural. That means
    they include people from more than one culture or race. Being
    multicultural has a lot of benefits. However, it also **presents** some
5   challenges.

    Immigrants aid their new homes in many ways. They offer fresh
    sources of **labor**, skills, and ideas. Some countries, including the USA
    and UK, **welcome** many immigrants every year.

    Yet, multicultural countries also face problems. One of the biggest
10 is with communication. It's not always easy for immigrants to **pick
    up** another language. That can make it hard to **get along with native**
    speakers. To **help out**, some governments run classes to teach the
    official language.

    Cultural issues also present
15 challenges. People often want
    to preserve the culture they
    grew up with. So, for example,
    many cities have Chinatowns.
    People also celebrate **holidays**
20 from their cultures. Critics feel
    the mainstream culture should
    receive more **attention**.

    Multiculturalism is a quickly growing trend. That's the case from
    North America to Europe to Asia. For example, in Korea, there are
25 already more than one million non-Korean residents. And, more
    than ten percent of new marriages are between Koreans and non-
    Koreans. Such situations present big challenges. They may take a
    long time to solve.

---

20 critics – people who are against something
21 mainstream – common; most widely practiced
25 residents – people living in a place

Questions about the Reading
Choose the best answer.

1. ( ) What is the main idea?
    (A) Multiculturalism is decreasing around the world.
    (B) Multiculturalism causes problems for governments.
    (C) Multiculturalism presents benefits and challenges.
    (D) Multiculturalism helps countries like the USA.

2. ( ) According to the article, how do immigrants help their new countries?
    (A) By offering labor and new ideas
    (B) By celebrating holidays from their cultures
    (C) By marrying native speakers
    (D) By offering language classes

3. ( ) What is NOT mentioned as a challenge faced by immigrants?
    (A) Learning a new language
    (B) Getting along with native speakers
    (C) Returning to their homelands for holidays
    (D) Preserving their culture

4. ( ) What does the word *trend* in line 23 mean?
    (A) challenge
    (B) culture
    (C) reason
    (D) movement

5. ( ) What does the article imply about marriages in Korea?
    (A) More than one million take place yearly.
    (B) More than half of them eventually fail.
    (C) More than one out of ten are multicultural.
    (D) More than 90% are very expensive to hold.

Writing about the Article
Answer each question based on the article.

1. What are two countries that welcome many immigrants every year?
    Many immigrants _____.

2. What can governments do to help immigrants?
    Governments can help by _____.

3. What do immigrants do to preserve their culture?
    Immigrants often _____.

Vocabulary Building — Choose the best word to fill in each blank.

1. _____ speakers should be patient with people who are learning the language.
   (A) Hard   (B) National   (C) Native   (D) Official

2. Ryan's favorite _____ is Thanksgiving because he gets to spend time with his family.
   (A) holiday   (B) attention   (C) challenge   (D) culture

3. A lot of new _____ to this country shop at the international supermarket.
   (A) critics   (B) cities   (C) benefits   (D) immigrants

4. Young children should receive support and _____ from their parents.
   (A) attention   (B) problems   (C) sources   (D) prevention

5. Building a house requires a lot of time and _____.
   (A) marriage   (B) labor   (C) trend   (D) percent

6. Warm weather _____ residents with a chance to spend time outdoors.
   (A) runs   (B) presents   (C) solves   (D) preserves

7. The two _____ languages of Canada are French and English. All government forms must be in both languages.
   (A) immigrant   (B) fresh   (C) cultural   (D) official

8. My relatives _____ us into their home when we visited Greece.
   (A) became   (B) aided   (C) welcomed   (D) included

Phrase Building — Write the correct phrase in each blank. (Remember to use the correct word form.)

● get along with   ● help out   ● pick up   ● grow up with

My friend Jari immigrated here from Finland. At first, we didn't have anything in common. He couldn't speak English, so I _____ at school. I made sure he understood the homework, and I introduced him to our classmates. After a few months, he _____ enough English to get by on his own. His family taught me a lot about the culture of Finland. Jari and I still _____ each other very well. We do everything together.

Grammar Exercise

Present Perfect

Complete each sentence using the present perfect tense.

Example: John and Tina _____ (live) there for three years.
Answer: John and Tina *have lived* there for three years.

1. Several of my friends _____ (eat) at this restaurant.

2. I'm so tired. I _____ (sleep) for nearly two days.

3. I love that movie. I _____ (see) it four times.

4. Jack, _____ (read) this article? It's really interesting.

5. No, she _____ (return) home yet. I'm a little worried.

Listening Exercise Track 32

Listen to the conversation. Then, answer the following questions.

1. (   ) Where was the man?
   - (A) At a Brazilian store
   - (B) At the neighbors' house
   - (C) At the supermarket
   - (D) At a computer shop

2. (   ) What will take place tomorrow night?
   - (A) A trip
   - (B) A move
   - (C) A sporting event
   - (D) A barbecue

3. (   ) What is the woman probably going to do next?
   - (A) Turn on her computer
   - (B) Go for a walk
   - (C) Visit her neighbors
   - (D) Call a travel agent

Listening Activity 🔘 Track 33

Listen to the description. Then, fill in the information in the chart.

1. What must students do before taking a free class?	
2. What scores qualify for the beginner class?	
3. What scores qualify for the intermediate class?	
4. What scores qualify for the advanced class?	
5. When are free classes held?	

Discussion Questions

1. Is your country multicultural? If so, in what ways? If not, what can it do to become more multicultural?

2. Do you think immigrants should completely leave their culture behind after moving to a new country? Why or why not?

3. What can people do to help immigrants adapt to their new home?

Discussion Activity

Imagine you and several classmates are going to emigrate to a new country. Which country will you choose? Why will you choose that place? What will you bring from your homeland? What will be hard about adapting to the new country?

Example: We are going to emigrate to Italy. We chose Italy because it has nice weather and delicious food....

Pre-Reading Questions Discuss these questions in pairs.

1. How do busy men and women meet new people?

2. What do people talk about the first time they meet?

3. Have you ever heard of speed dating?

Consider the Topic Read each statement. Check if you agree or disagree with it.

	agree	disagree
1. Working (or studying) takes up most of my time.	☐	☐
2. It's hard for people to meet men and women that they're compatible with.	☐	☐
3. I know if I like someone after talking with him or her for a few minutes.	☐	☐

Reading Passage Track 34

1 These days, people are busier than ever. We're always looking for new **methods** to save time. That includes meeting people. Speed dating is a new way to meet many people in a short period of time.

Speed dating is simple. First, **single** men and women sign up for
5 a local **event**. That's usually done online, through a company that hosts these events.

At an event, there are usually 10-20 men and an **equal** number of women. During each "mini date," a man and woman **chat** for a set period of time (usually from 3-8 minutes). When time is up, a bell
10 rings. Then, each man **switches** tables and talks to another woman until the next bell rings. **In this way**, all the single people have a chance to meet each other.

After the event, participants **fill out** cards. They mark which people they are interested
15 in. If two people want to see each other again, that's a match. The host of the event sends contact **information** to each person in a match. They can then contact each other to **set up** a longer date.

20 There are speed dating events in many countries, from England to Australia to Taiwan. It's a 21st **century** way to meet Mr. or Ms. Right.

4 sign up – register
13 participants – people who take part in an event
22 Mr. or Ms. Right – the perfect man or woman for you

Questions about the Reading   Choose the best answer.

1. (   ) What is the main idea?
   - (A) At least 10 people attend most speed dating events.
   - (B) Speed dating is a fast way for people to meet each other.
   - (C) These days, people's lives are busier than ever.
   - (D) Young people have very different lives from their parents.

2. (   ) Which of the following is true about speed dating events?
   - (A) Most mini dates last more than 8 minutes.
   - (B) People can sign up for events on the Internet.
   - (C) There are always 30 people at an event.
   - (D) The women switch tables when the bell rings.

3. (   ) What happens last at a speed dating event?
   - (A) A bell rings and people switch tables.
   - (B) Everyone fills out a card.
   - (C) Men and women have mini dates.
   - (D) Participants sign up online.

4. (   ) Who sends out contact information to event participants?
   - (A) Every person who attends
   - (B) Only the men who are there
   - (C) People who want to meet again
   - (D) The host of the event

5. (   ) What does the word *period* in line 9 mean?
   - (A) mark
   - (B) hour
   - (C) length
   - (D) discussion

Writing about the Article   Answer each question based on the article.

1. At speed dating events, how long do mini dates last?

   Mini dates usually _____ .

2. What do participants mark on the cards?

   On the cards, participants _____ .

3. What are some countries with speed dating events?

   There are events _____ .

69

Vocabulary Building   Choose the best word to fill in each blank.

1. This house was built more than a _____ ago.
   (A) period   (B) century   (C) date   (D) time

2. Now that I'm _____ again, my friends keep introducing me to girls!
   (A) simple   (B) equal   (C) short   (D) single

3. Let's get some coffee this afternoon and _____ about things then.
   (A) chat   (B) mark   (C) ring   (D) contact

4. What's the best _____ for growing vegetables in a small garden?
   (A) match   (B) minute   (C) method   (D) number

5. You have to go to the dance. It's the most important _____ of the year.
   (A) event   (B) bell   (C) host   (D) participant

6. If your cell phone service is that bad, you should _____ companies.
   (A) meet   (B) ring   (C) include   (D) switch

7. On the website, you'll find all the _____ you need about the college.
   (A) way   (B) information   (C) date   (D) chance

8. For this dessert, add a(n) _____ amount of chocolate and strawberry ice cream.
   (A) another   (B) equal   (C) next   (D) each

Phrase Building   Write the correct phrase in each blank. (Remember to use the correct word form.)

● fill out   ● in this way   ● talk to   ● set up

Since all my friends have blogs, I decided to start one. I thought it would be hard to _____, but it was actually pretty easy. I just went onto a famous website for blogs and _____ a short form. I like cats, so I chose Cat Corner for my blog name. In less than 10 minutes, I posted my first article! Now I post something every day. _____, people will know it's a serious blog and will keep reading it.

Grammar Exercise

All, Every, and None

Complete each sentence with *all*, *every*, **or** *none*.

> **Example:** _____ seat was taken, so we went to another coffee shop.
>
> **Answer:** *Every* seat was taken, so we went to another coffee shop.

1. Are these _____ of the bags? Isn't there one more?

2. _____ of us has a membership card. We can't get a store discount.

3. I believe _____ bus goes by the train station.

4. Since _____ of my friends spoke Spanish, we had some language problems during the trip.

5. _____ set meal comes with a drink and dessert.

Listening Exercise Track 35

Listen to the conversation. Then, answer the following questions.

1. (   ) When will the event be held?
   (A) Tonight
   (B) Tomorrow
   (C) The following Friday
   (D) Two weeks from now

2. (   ) Why doesn't the woman want to try speed dating?
   (A) She thinks the men might be strange.
   (B) She already has a boyfriend.
   (C) She has a test on the day of the event.
   (D) She never has luck with speed dating.

3. (   ) How does the man try to convince the woman?
   (A) By telling her about his experiences
   (B) By making sure she feels safe
   (C) By offering to give her a ride home
   (D) By suggesting that she skip her test

Listening Activity Track 36

Listen to the advertisement. Then, fill in the information in the chart.

1. When will the event be held?	
2. What is the Perfect Shot?	
3. Where can people register?	
4. What is the charge?	
5. What does the charge include?	

Discussion Questions

1. What attracts you the most to another person? (appearance? personality?)

2. Is five minutes enough time to get a good idea about a person? Why or why not?

3. What kinds of things would you NOT tell someone at a speed dating event? (For example, would you talk about your salary?)

Discussion Activity

See how quickly you can learn about your classmates. First, write down three questions you would normally ask a new friend. Then, take turns asking your questions to several classmates. (Only spend 3-5 minutes talking to each classmate.) After you're done, try to tell the whole class about one of your classmates.

Example: **Student A**: What kind of work do you do?

Student B: Right now, I'm a university student.

Discuss these questions in pairs.

1. What are the biggest cities in your country?

2. What places in your city do tourists love visiting?

3. What are some of your country's important industries?

Consider the Topic Read each statement. Check if you agree or disagree with it.

	agree	disagree
1. I think about the future a lot.	☐	☐
2. Shanghai would be an interesting place to visit.	☐	☐
3. Cities should have many cultural sites, like museums and theaters.	☐	☐

Reading Passage 🔘 Track 37

1　Shanghai is often called the city of the future. Thousands of skyscrapers rise above the city. They hold the offices of **major** companies from **Asia**, Europe, North America, and elsewhere. The city is also a cultural center, bringing in large numbers of visitors.

5　For good reason, Shanghai's 18 million **residents** are **proud of** their home.

China's largest city, Shanghai is **located** at the mouth of the Yangtze River. That puts it in an excellent spot for trading. The city's yearly foreign **trade** totals hundreds of billions of dollars. And, its port is

10　now the world's largest.

The area around Shanghai **supports** companies making many different products. Factories make cars, electronics, and medicines, **to name a few**. Foreign investors are **pouring money into** local projects. Germany, Japan, Singapore, and the USA have all been big investors.

15　But Shanghai is not all about business. It's famous for its music, **museums**, and theaters. The Yuyuan garden attracts many guests. Tourists also love visiting the Bund, a walking area along the

20　Huangpu River.

Visitors to Shanghai often talk about the feeling of excitement there. It's a city full of energy and hope. The **host** of the 2010 World Expo, Shanghai is running towards

25　the future as fast as it can.

---

² skyscraper – very tall building
⁴ bring in – attract
⁹ port – place (near land) where boats park
¹³ investor – person who spends money on a project or company
　(with the goal of making more money)

Questions about the Reading

Choose the best answer.

1. (   ) According to the article, what is a big help to Shanghai's foreign trade?
   - (A) Its location
   - (B) Its size
   - (C) Its population
   - (D) Its tourists

2. (   ) In Shanghai, what is the Yuyuan garden a good example of?
   - (A) The city's cultural side
   - (B) The city's foreign trade
   - (C) The city's local industries
   - (D) The city's new buildings

3. (   ) What would you NOT expect Shanghai's factories to make?
   - (A) Radios
   - (B) Sofas
   - (C) Aspirin
   - (D) Trucks

4. (   ) Which of the following is true?
   - (A) At this time, there are no car factories near Shanghai.
   - (B) No cities in China are larger than Shanghai.
   - (C) The Yuyuan garden is beside the Huangpu River.
   - (D) Shanghai's foreign trade is only worth 100 million dollars.

5. (   ) What does the word *mouth* in line 7 mean?
   - (A) state
   - (B) water
   - (C) opening
   - (D) port

Writing about the Article

Answer each question based on the article.

1. How many people live in Shanghai?

   There are _____.

2. What countries are big investors in Shanghai?

   Some big investors are _____.

3. Where is the Bund located?

   It is located _____.

Vocabulary Building Choose the best word to fill in each blank.

1. Hasbro is a _____ toy company. It's one of the world's largest.
   (A) major   (B) cultural   (C) fast   (D) future

2. I _____ your decision to change jobs. You should be happy with your work.
   (A) total   (B) put   (C) support   (D) hold

3. At the history _____, there are many 500-year-old items on display.
   (A) museum   (B) industry   (C) garden   (D) factory

4. The bank is _____ across the street from the library.
   (A) famous   (B) large   (C) located   (D) full

5. You have to be a(n) _____ of this neighborhood to park your car here.
   (A) center   (B) office   (C) reason   (D) resident

6. The party's _____ thanked everyone for visiting his home.
   (A) investor   (B) host   (C) tourist   (D) guest

7. China is the largest country in _____.
   (A) Europe   (B) Asia   (C) Shanghai   (D) North America

8. International _____ allows countries to buy what they need from other countries.
   (A) trade   (B) port   (C) theater   (D) skyscraper

Phrase Building Write the correct phrase in each blank.

● proud of   ● full of   ● to name a few   ● pour money into

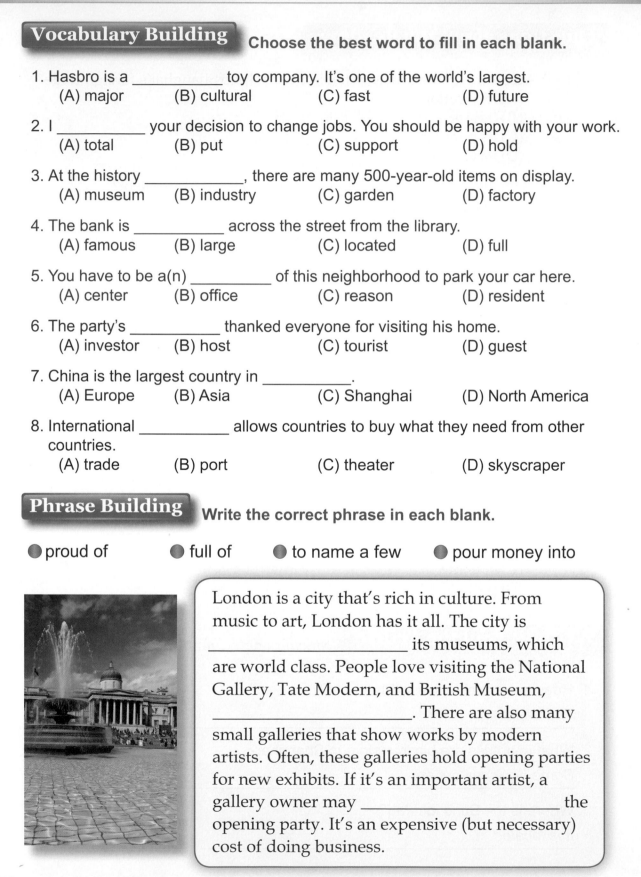

London is a city that's rich in culture. From music to art, London has it all. The city is _____ its museums, which are world class. People love visiting the National Gallery, Tate Modern, and British Museum, _____. There are also many small galleries that show works by modern artists. Often, these galleries hold opening parties for new exhibits. If it's an important artist, a gallery owner may _____ the opening party. It's an expensive (but necessary) cost of doing business.

Grammar Exercise

Prepositions of Place

Choose the correct word to complete each sentence.

Example: There are several music stores (in/along) this street.
Answer: There are several music stores (in/along) this street.

1. Put the red chair (beside/next) the table.

2. The post office is (in/inside) between a movie theater and a bookstore.

3. My car is parked (across/around) the corner.

4. Some people are playing music (under/among) the bridge.

5. Our cat likes to sit (at/on) top of the car.

Listening Exercise   Track 38

Listen to the conversation. Then, answer the following questions.

1. (   ) How was Lily's experience in Shanghai?
    (A) It was exactly like she expected.
    (B) The city was a big surprise to her.
    (C) She didn't have time to see much.
    (D) Her tour guide planned everything.

2. (   ) What did Lily think the city would be like?
    (A) Modern
    (B) Exciting
    (C) Cheap
    (D) Crowded

3. (   ) Who will travel to Shanghai soon?
    (A) George
    (B) The woman
    (C) George's sister
    (D) The woman's boss

77

Listening Activity ◎ Track 39

Listen to the report. Then, fill in the information in the chart.

1. What is happening to Shanghai?	
2. What are travelers reporting?	
3. What do many people complain about?	
4. Who is happy about the situation?	
5. Who is spending a lot at shops?	

Discussion Questions

1. If you could take a trip around China, where would you go? What would you like to see?

2. Many of the world's biggest cities – Paris, Shanghai, and so on – are near rivers and oceans. Why are such locations important to cities?

3. In many countries, fewer and fewer people are living in the countryside. More and more people are moving to cities. Why do you think that is?

Discussion Activity

Shanghai is one gateway into the huge China market. Imagine you are going to do business in China, starting with opening an office in Shanghai. What kinds of goods or services will you sell? Will it be something from your country or something totally new?

Example: We're going to start a t-shirt business. We think many young people in Shanghai and other cities in China will like them. The shirts will be designed by people in my country....

1. In your country, is global warming a big topic in the news?

2. Does it feel like your country is getting hotter?

3. Are you worried about global warming?

Consider the Topic Read each statement. Check if you agree or disagree with it.

	agree	disagree
1. Global warming will affect all of our lives.	☐	☐
2. It is the government's job to stop global warming.	☐	☐
3. There's nothing I can do to help solve the problem.	☐	☐

Reading Passage 🔘 Track 40

1   Power plants, factories, and cars are the main causes of global warming. They release pollution into the air, trapping the sun's heat. That **causes** the Earth's temperature to rise, **leading to** many problems. Indeed, fighting global warming may be the biggest
5   **challenge** of our time.

As **temperatures** rise, so do sea levels. If they become too high, they could flood cities near the ocean. Warmer temperatures also make storms like typhoons more serious. And, a hotter planet may cause many animals and plants to become extinct.

10   There is good news. We have the technology to **slow down** global warming. New equipment can lower the pollution from power plants. Also, car makers can use new technology to make engines cleaner. Plus, we can get more **energy** from wind, solar, and other **clean** sources.

15   New laws are needed to make these changes happen. However, some **governments** worry that such laws will hurt their economies. Getting the world's governments to
20   **agree** on the issue is not easy.

People like you and me can help in the fight. **For example**, buy refrigerators and light bulbs that use less energy. Also, when buying
25   a new car, **consider** one with a hybrid engine. By working together, it is possible to slow down global warming.

---

2 trap – keep from getting out
7 flood – cover with water
9 extinct – totally gone, with none left
12 engine – machine that gives a car power
13 solar – coming from the sun
25 hybrid engine – engine that uses both gasoline and electricity

Questions about the Reading
Choose the best answer.

1. (   ) What is the main idea?
  (A) We need to work together to fight global warming.
  (B) Global warming will mostly affect plants and animals.
  (C) It may not be possible to slow down global warming.
  (D) Governments are not doing enough about global warming.

2. (   ) Which of the following is NOT caused by global warming?
  (A) Rising sea levels
  (B) More serious storms
  (C) Animal species disappearing
  (D) Fruit growing in size

3. (   ) Why is it hard to get governments to pass new laws?
  (A) They don't have anybody's support.
  (B) They don't care about the environment.
  (C) They don't want to hurt their economies.
  (D) They don't know which laws to pass.

4. (   ) How are people like you and me encouraged to help?
  (A) By passing new laws
  (B) By replacing power plant equipment
  (C) By using less energy
  (D) By building cleaner engines

5. (   ) What does the word *issue* in line 20 mean?
  (A) pass
  (B) matter
  (C) release
  (D) copy

Writing about the Article
Answer each question based on the article.

1. What is causing global warming?

   Mainly, power plants _____ .

2. What are some clean sources of energy?

   Some clean energy sources _____ .

3. What type of car can help in the fight against global warming?

   Cars with _____ .

Vocabulary Building Choose the best word to fill in each blank.

1. Let's _____ on a place to go on vacation. Then, we'll call a travel agent.
   (A) agree   (B) become   (C) make   (D) release

2. Building a new school will be a big _____. The city may not have enough money.
   (A) challenge   (B) government   (C) economy   (D) technology

3. We have guests coming over, so I want the living room to be very _____.
   (A) easy   (B) possible   (C) clean   (D) high

4. The city _____ has done a great job building new parks. There are now parks in almost every neighborhood.
   (A) economy   (B) government   (C) pollution   (D) factory

5. I wonder what's _____ all this traffic.
   (A) lowering   (B) happening   (C) getting   (D) causing

6. Bring a jacket. The _____ is supposed to fall this afternoon.
   (A) equipment   (B) heat   (C) energy   (D) temperature

7. The company will _____ your idea. But, I'm not sure if they will accept it.
   (A) trap   (B) consider   (C) rise   (D) cause

8. Air conditioners use a lot of _____ to keep your house cool.
   (A) energy   (B) laws   (C) news   (D) pollution

Phrase Building Write the correct phrase in each blank.

● slow down   ● for example   ● worry about   ● lead to

My friends and I love eating cake. Every week, our Dessert Club tries out a new place. _____, last week, we went across the city for some chocolate cake. It was so good! My sister says I eat too much junk food. She thinks the Dessert Club should _____ its meeting schedule to once or twice a month. I know eating junk food can _____ weight gain. But like I told my sister, I exercise a lot, so I think I'm healthy.

Grammar Exercise

Modals

Complete each sentence with the correct choice.

Example: My brother is very smart. He (can/could) speak four languages.

Answer: My brother is very smart. He (can)/could) speak four languages.

1. I (will/would) buy you a CD if I have enough money.

2. It's getting cold. You (shall/should) probably wear a jacket.

3. Yes, Timothy is here. (May/Must) I ask who's calling?

4. They were sold out, so we (can't/couldn't) get one.

5. We (must/might) leave right now. Let's go.

Listening Exercise   Track 41

Listen to the conversation. Then, answer the following questions.

1. (   ) Why is the woman unsure about getting a hybrid car?
    (A) The cars are very hard to find.
    (B) It would cost a lot to buy one.
    (C) She thinks gas is too expensive.
    (D) Her friend told her it's a bad idea.

2. (   ) What does the man suggest about hybrid cars?
    (A) They are worth buying.
    (B) They are definitely a waste of money.
    (C) They are good for the environment.
    (D) They are becoming popular.

3. (   ) What does the woman want the man to do?
    (A) Tell her about his car
    (B) Help her choose a model
    (C) Show her an article
    (D) Go car shopping with her

Listening Activity 🔘 Track 42

Listen to the report. Then, fill in the information in the chart.

1. What will storms be like this summer?	
2. What is causing that to happen?	
3. What are the months of the storm season?	
4. What should people have ready?	
5. What should people listen closely to?	

Discussion Questions

1. It seems many people don't worry about global warming. Why is it so hard to get people to pay attention to the issue?

2. What can you do in your own life to create less pollution and use less energy?

3. Some poor countries say they can't afford to stop using dirty energy sources (like coal). They say rich countries should do more to fight global warming. Do you agree with this point of view?

Discussion Activity

Businesses worry that buying "clean" equipment is too expensive. People worried about the environment say the cost is worth it. Divide into groups of four, with two students on each side of the issue. Each side should list the reasons for its point of view. Then, try to find a solution that everybody in the group can agree on.

Example: We represent our country's businesses. If we have to buy new equipment, we will lose money. First we will have to fire people. Then we will have to raise the cost of our products....

Pre-Reading Questions
Discuss these questions in pairs.

1. How do you usually travel between cities? (car? bus? train?)

2. Have you ever taken a high speed train?

3. Would you feel safe traveling at 300 kilometers per hour?

Consider the Topic
Read each statement. Check if you agree or disagree with it.

	agree	disagree
1. Using public transportation is better than using private cars.	☐	☐
2. When going on a trip, I would rather take a plane than a train.	☐	☐
3. My country should build more high speed train lines.	☐	☐

Reading Passage Track 43

1   Trains have long been an **important** form of **transportation**. Yet they have changed a lot since 1804, when the first train moved

5   at 8 km/hr. Today's high speed trains can go 300 km/hr or faster. **Besides** their speed, they have many **advantages** over other transportation types.

10   Japan built the world's first high speed railway. In 1964, Japan's "shinkansen" trains started **traveling** between Osaka and Tokyo at 200 km/hr. Over time, more lines, **as well as** faster trains, were **built**.

15   Many other countries, including Korea, England, and the USA, now have their own high speed **systems**. Taiwan's started running in 2007. Its trains are **based on** two types of shinkansen trains. They can carry 989 people and travel from Taipei to Kaohsiung in less than two hours!

20   These systems are expensive to build, but they have many advantages. For example, they are good for the environment. Trains on the London to Paris line create 1/10 the pollution that planes create. High speed trains are also **safer** and cleaner than cars.

    Super fast trains can even help a country's economy. They make it
25   easier to travel to **far away** places. That helps businesses and land values in those areas. It's no wonder so many countries are building their own high speed railways.

⁵ km – kilometer (1 kilometer equals 0.62 miles)
¹¹ railway – train system
²² create – make
²⁶ no wonder – not surprising

Questions about the Reading   Choose the best answer.

1. (   ) What is the main idea?
   - (A) Trains are the world's most popular form of transportation.
   - (B) It used to take a long time to go from Taipei to Kaohsiung.
   - (C) We should do everything we can to help the environment.
   - (D) There are many good reasons to build high speed railways.

2. (   ) When was the world's first high speed railway built?
   - (A) 1804
   - (B) 1904
   - (C) 1964
   - (D) 2007

3. (   ) In Taiwan, the high speed trains are based on trains from which country?
   - (A) Korea
   - (B) England
   - (C) Japan
   - (D) The USA

4. (   ) What is NOT an advantage of high speed trains?
   - (A) They are very cheap to build.
   - (B) They are safer than other transportation types.
   - (C) They don't create a lot of pollution.
   - (D) They are good for a country's businesses.

5. (   ) What does the word *value* in line 26 mean?
   - (A) help
   - (B) result
   - (C) price
   - (D) enjoyment

Writing about the Article   Answer each question based on the article.

1. How fast did Japan's first shinkansen go?

   The first shinkansen _____.

2. How many people can travel on Taiwan's high speed trains?

   Each train can _____.

3. How long does the high speed train from Taipei to Kaohsiung take?

   The train takes _____.

Vocabulary Building — Choose the best word to fill in each blank.

1. Is it _____ to pet your dog? I'm worried he might bite me.
   (A) clean　　(B) easy　　(C) safe　　(D) fast

2. They need to _____ larger roads. There are too many cars going down these old roads.
   (A) build　　(B) wonder　　(C) travel　　(D) carry

3. _____ a new TV, we're thinking of getting a new sofa.
   (A) Yet　　(B) Indeed　　(C) Besides　　(D) Over

4. One nice _____ of taking a train is you can sleep during the ride.
   (A) advantage　(B) value　　(C) type　　(D) example

5. Summer is the most popular month for people to _____. Lots of families take trips together then.
   (A) travel　　(B) move　　(C) start　　(D) change

6. Our education _____ is great. The schools and teachers are excellent.
   (A) country　　(B) economy　　(C) system　　(D) line

7. That information isn't _____. You don't need to write it down.
   (A) important　(B) expensive　(C) own　　(D) long

8. Many students love to ride bicycles. It's a popular form of _____.
   (A) railway　　(B) transportation　(C) business　　(D) environment

Phrase Building — Write the correct phrase in each blank.

● over time　　● far away　　● as well as　　● based on

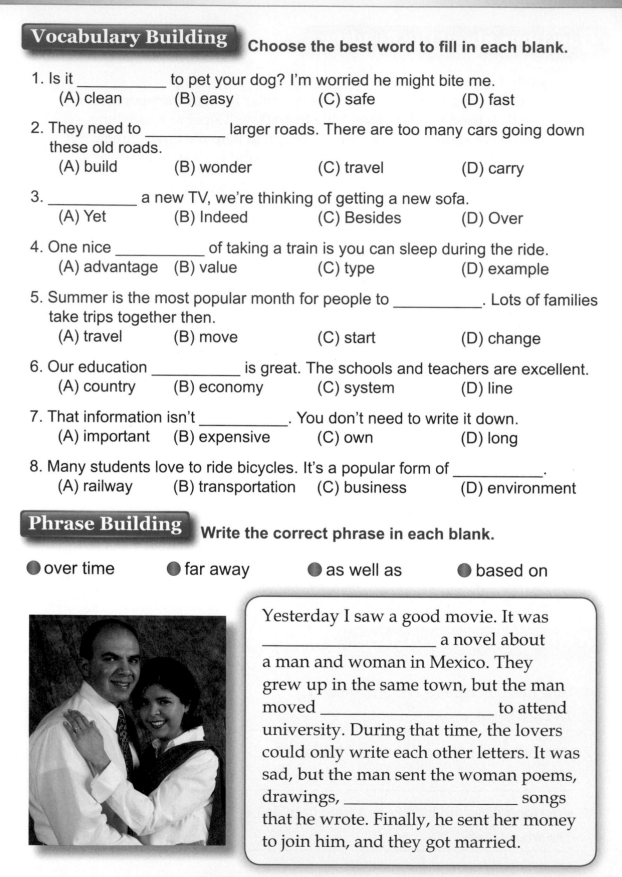

Yesterday I saw a good movie. It was _____ a novel about a man and woman in Mexico. They grew up in the same town, but the man moved _____ to attend university. During that time, the lovers could only write each other letters. It was sad, but the man sent the woman poems, drawings, _____ songs that he wrote. Finally, he sent her money to join him, and they got married.

Grammar Exercise

Pronouns

Complete each sentence with the correct word.

Example: The car belongs to (he/him/his).
Answer: The car belongs to (he/him/his).

1. Are you sure this bag is (she/her/hers)?

2. When Martha gets home, please tell (she/her/herself) I called.

3. All of (us/our/ourselves) agree with the decision.

4. One of (they/them/their) salespeople will come by today.

5. If it isn't (you/your/yours), whose is it?

Listening Exercise   Track 44

Listen to the conversation. Then, answer the following questions.

1. (   ) How much does the train cost?
   (A) 400 NT *
   (B) 500 NT
   (C) 1,500 NT
   (D) 2,000 NT

2. (   ) What is important to the woman?
   (A) Arriving in Kaohsiung on time
   (B) Saving as much money as possible
   (C) Having something to do during the trip
   (D) Taking a quiet form of transportation

3. (   ) What advantage does the bus have?
   (A) It has television sets on board.
   (B) It is faster than the train.
   (C) It doesn't have to deal with traffic.
   (D) It offers the best views.

* NT = New Taiwan dollars (the currency of Taiwan)

Listening Activity   Track 45

Listen to the report. Then, fill in the information in the chart.

1. How many people did the reporter talk to?	
2. What percentage of people thought the trains saved time?	
3. How did people describe the trains?	
4. What did people complain about?	
5. How many people made that complaint?	

Discussion Questions

1. Rather than use public transportation systems, many people still prefer to drive private cars. Why is that?

2. What special services would you like to see on trains? (food car? game car? movie car?)

3. If you could take a high speed train trip in a foreign country, where would it be? What would you like to see in the country?

Discussion Activity

Your country wants to improve its public transportation system. The system will have two parts: one for getting around your city, and one for traveling between the main cities. Working in small groups, decide which types of transportation projects to build.

Example: Our city already has a subway system, but we can make it bigger and faster. Also, tickets are too expensive, so we would like to lower their cost....

Pre-Reading Questions

Discuss these questions in pairs.

1. How many brothers and sisters do you have?

2. How many children would you like to have?

3. What is a good age to get married?

Consider the Topic

Read each statement. Check if you agree or disagree with it.

	agree	disagree
1. Most of my friends only plan to have one child.	☐	☐
2. It's very expensive to raise children.	☐	☐
3. Children with no brothers or sisters usually grow up lonely.	☐	☐

Reading Passage 💿 Track 46

1   Modern families are very different from the families of 50 years ago. Fewer **relatives** live together, and people are having fewer children. Single child families, once **unusual**, are becoming **common**.

5   Money is a big **reason** for the shrinking family size. Education, health care, and other costs are rising every year. One study in the USA **added it up**. It found the cost to **raise** a child (from birth to 18 years of age) to be about $300,000.

Another study in Australia showed that married
10   couples often want several children. However, the husband and wife usually both work. They have time and money **pressures**.
15   That makes it hard to raise a large family.

Also, people in many countries are getting married later in life. Many women have their first child when they're 35 or older. At that age, it can be hard to have a second child.

20   **On the plus side**, in single child families, parents' time and money go **towards** just one child. On the minus side, parents often worry about their son or daughter being lonely. However, by spending time with friends, such problems can be overcome. Indeed, studies show that only children usually **grow up** happily, just like children
25   with one or more **siblings**.

⁴ shrinking – becoming smaller
²¹ minus – bad; negative
²³ overcome – dealt with; solved
²⁴ only children – children with no brothers or sisters

Questions about the Reading
Choose the best answer.

1. (   ) What is the main idea?
    (A) There are many reasons why families have just one child.
    (B) In 50 years, families will be even smaller.
    (C) A lot of people get married after they're 30 years old.
    (D) Raising an only child is very hard work.

2. (   ) How do money issues affect the American family size?
    (A) All costs except education keep rising.
    (B) Children don't start working until they're 18.
    (C) Relatives living with families don't help out.
    (D) $300,000 is a lot of money to raise a child.

3. (   ) Why do many Australian families have just one child?
    (A) The couples don't want more than one child.
    (B) Usually, only the husband or the wife works.
    (C) They are worried about the costs and time needed.
    (D) There are laws against having several children.

4. (   ) What does the article suggest about women over 35 years of age?
    (A) They often like to focus on their work.
    (B) They may have problems having a second child.
    (C) They have a lot of experience raising children.
    (D) They like to wait a few years before getting married.

5. (   ) What do studies say about children without siblings?
    (A) Such children usually have happy lives.
    (B) They have a hard time meeting other children.
    (C) The children often worry about their parents.
    (D) Their biggest problem is growing up lonely.

Writing about the Article
Answer each question based on the article.

1. What does the article suggest about families from 50 years ago?
    At that time, more relatives   .
    _____

2. In Australian families, who usually works?
    Usually in Australia, the   .
    _____

3. How do only children overcome being lonely?
    They can spend   .
    _____

Vocabulary Building — Choose the best word to fill in each blank.

1. Those little red birds are _____ in this area. We see them all the time.
    (A) single   (B) modern   (C) hard   (D) common

2. Please write down your name and _____ for visiting the building.
    (A) reason   (B) problem   (C) size   (D) age

3. Students are under a lot of _____. They have to do homework every day and take many tests.
    (A) time   (B) education   (C) pressure   (D) cost

4. All my time is going _____ my work. It's very important to me.
    (A) about   (B) towards   (C) usually   (D) often

5. Children like to _____ pets like dogs and cats.
    (A) add   (B) raise   (C) spend   (D) live

6. We have _____ in Sydney. We stay at their house when we're in town.
    (A) couples   (B) reasons   (C) ages   (D) relatives

7. That's a(n) _____ hat. I've never seen anything like it before.
    (A) unusual   (B) single   (C) lonely   (D) late

8. I have two _____: one brother and one sister.
    (A) families   (B) children   (C) siblings   (D) parents

Phrase Building — Write the correct phrase in each blank. (Remember to use the correct word form.)

● on the plus side   ● add up   ● spend time with   ● grow up

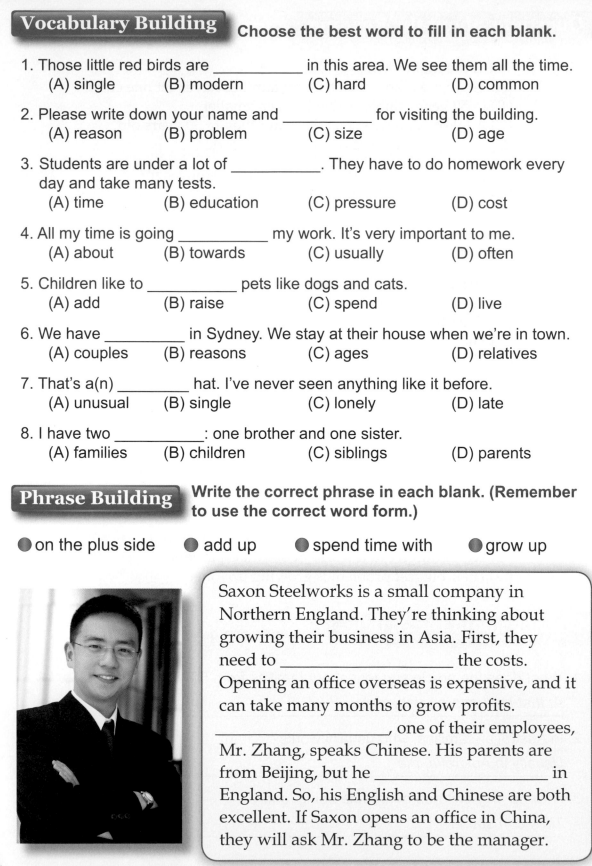

Saxon Steelworks is a small company in Northern England. They're thinking about growing their business in Asia. First, they need to _____ the costs. Opening an office overseas is expensive, and it can take many months to grow profits. _____, one of their employees, Mr. Zhang, speaks Chinese. His parents are from Beijing, but he _____ in England. So, his English and Chinese are both excellent. If Saxon opens an office in China, they will ask Mr. Zhang to be the manager.

Grammar Exercise

Prepositions of Time

Complete each sentence with *at*, *in*, **or** *on*.

Example: _____ his age, it's hard to walk around a lot.
Answer: *At* his age, it's hard to walk around a lot.

1. _____ my 20th birthday, I went out with some friends.

2. My sister was born _____ 1980.

3. _____ this time, we're not ready to make a decision.

4. _____ my first year of college, I had a lot of homework.

5. Are you free _____ September 15th?

Listening Exercise Track 47

Listen to the conversation. Then, answer the following questions.

1. (   ) Who is Tim?
    (A) Linda's husband
    (B) Marge's brother
    (C) Steve's son
    (D) Kyle's father

2. (   ) What does NOT affect Steve's decision to have more children?
    (A) Space issues
    (B) Money issues
    (C) Time issues
    (D) Age issues

3. (   ) How does Marge feel about Steve's situation?
    (A) She knows how he feels.
    (B) She thinks he can solve his problems.
    (C) She doesn't understand him.
    (D) She disagrees with his decision.

Listening Activity ⊙ Track 48

Listen to the report. Then, fill in the information in the chart.

1. What industry is affected by smaller families?	
2. How many bedrooms did houses use to have?	
3. How many bedrooms do many new houses have?	
4. What do most children have?	
5. What did children do in the past?	

Discussion Questions

1. In many countries, there are fewer and fewer young people, and more and more older people. What problems does this situation create?

2. Some people decide to have children without getting married. How do you feel about that?

3. How do you feel about couples raising just one child? In your opinion, is it better for children to grow up with siblings?

Discussion Activity

Your government has decided that the population is getting too old. It wants to encourage people to have more children. Design a "Have More Children" campaign. How will you encourage people to have more kids?

Example: Since everyone cares about money, it will be important in our campaign. First, we will let mothers rest for six months after having a child. They will continue to receive their salaries while resting....

Pre-Reading Questions
Discuss these questions in pairs.

1. Do you often shop on the Internet? If so, how do you pay for things?

2. Look at the picture. What do you think is happening?

3. What could a thief do with your personal information?

Consider the Topic
Read each statement. Check if you agree or disagree with it.

	agree	disagree
1. I have a lot of credit cards.	☐	☐
2. I'm worried about someone stealing my personal information.	☐	☐
3. There are a lot of thieves on the Internet.	☐	☐

Reading Passage   ◎ Track 49

1   The modern world is very convenient. It's easy to buy or rent things. We can do a lot of our shopping and banking on the Internet. **However**, we also face a growing problem: identity theft.

    We often give our **personal** information to stores. That includes
5   our birth date, personal ID number, and home address. When we apply for a store membership, we give our information to a stranger. When buying something online, we do the same thing.

    Thieves work hard to get that information. They steal receipts and **break into** computers. They also try to steal our passwords.
10 Thieves can use that information to "become" another person. That's identity theft.

    One common **crime** is to **apply for** a credit card using someone else's name. The thief buys expensive things but doesn't pay the bill. That can hurt a victim's credit. With bad credit, it's harder to
15 get bank or car loans.

    How can you **prevent** identity theft? First, be careful about giving away personal information. Only give someone your birth date
20 and personal ID number when **necessary**. Second, tear up old credit card receipts and bank statements if you don't need them. Finally, some **experts recommend** paying in **cash**
25 **as much as possible**.

---

⁷ stranger – person that we do not know
⁸ thieves – people who steal things
¹⁴ victim – person who suffers from a crime
¹⁵ loan – money that you borrow

Questions about the Reading
Choose the best answer.

1. (   ) What is the main idea?
   - (A) Identity theft is the world's fastest-growing crime.
   - (B) There are many thieves on the Internet.
   - (C) Identity theft is common, but it can be prevented.
   - (D) Good credit is important for getting a car loan.

2. (   ) According to the article, what do thieves do with the information they steal?
   - (A) They apply for store memberships.
   - (B) They sell it on the Internet.
   - (C) They use it to get credit cards.
   - (D) They try to get bank loans.

3. (   ) Which of the following is true?
   - (A) Identity theft wasn't a problem a few years ago.
   - (B) Identity theft only happens to people with credit cards.
   - (C) Identity theft is hurting more and more people.
   - (D) Identity theft is usually caused by Internet shopping.

4. (   ) What does the word *they* in line 9 refer to?
   - (A) computers
   - (B) receipts
   - (C) thieves
   - (D) victims

5. (   ) How does the article suggest protecting yourself?
   - (A) By being careful when throwing away receipts
   - (B) By buying fewer things at small stores
   - (C) By keeping all of your bank statements
   - (D) By watching out for thieves when using cash

Writing about the Article
Answer each question based on the article.

1. What personal information do we often give out?

   We often give out our _____.

2. How do thieves try to get our information?

   They steal _____.

3. What problem may be faced by victims of identity theft?

   Identity theft can hurt _____.

Vocabulary Building

Choose the best word to fill in each blank.

1. You don't have to give me a ride home. It really isn't _____.
   (A) same   (B) necessary   (C) careful   (D) modern

2. Most days, I ride my bike to school. This morning, _____, I took the bus.
   (A) usually   (B) often   (C) every   (D) however

3. My brother is a car _____. He knows everything about them.
   (A) expert   (B) information   (C) identity   (D) victim

4. Wash your hands often. It will help _____ catching a cold.
   (A) prevent   (B) give   (C) recommend   (D) include

5. This is a safe town, with very little _____ or other problems.
   (A) loan   (B) membership   (C) crime   (D) address

6. Can you _____ a good eye doctor?
   (A) face   (B) rent   (C) give   (D) recommend

7. One of my e-mail accounts is for work. The other is for _____ e-mails, like writing to friends.
   (A) modern   (B) personal   (C) easy   (D) old

8. I don't have enough _____ with me. Can I pay with a credit card?
   (A) password   (B) cash   (C) bill   (D) receipt

Phrase Building

Write the correct phrase in each blank.

● as much as possible   ● tear up   ● apply for   ● break into

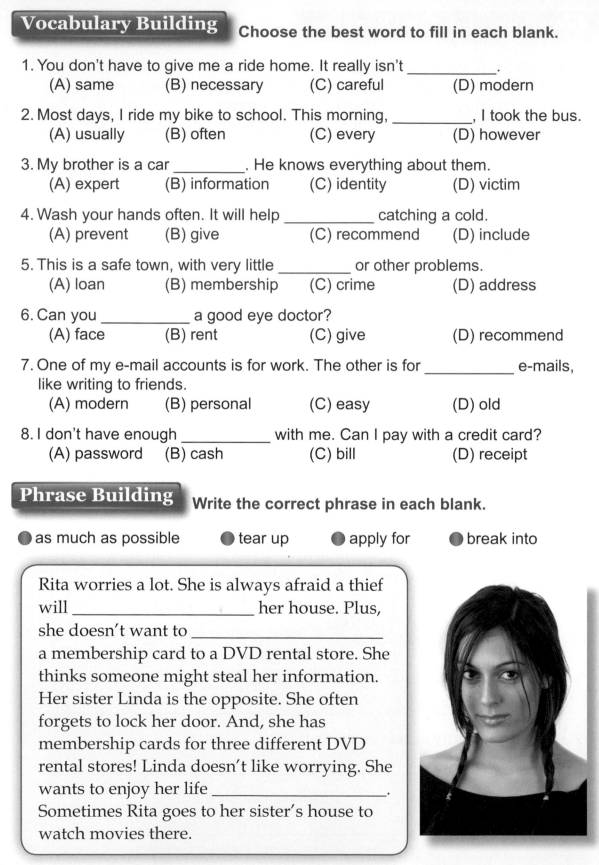

Rita worries a lot. She is always afraid a thief will _____ her house. Plus, she doesn't want to _____ a membership card to a DVD rental store. She thinks someone might steal her information. Her sister Linda is the opposite. She often forgets to lock her door. And, she has membership cards for three different DVD rental stores! Linda doesn't like worrying. She wants to enjoy her life _____. Sometimes Rita goes to her sister's house to watch movies there.

Grammar Exercise

Making Comparisons

Complete each sentence with the correct form of the word.

Example: The music is (loud) _____ than it should be.

Answer: The music is *louder* than it should be.

1. I go to sleep (early) _____ than my sister.

2. This Italian restaurant is more (expensive) _____ than the one near my house.

3. Tokyo gets (cold) _____ than Hong Kong in winter.

4. Can you really run (fast) _____ than Jack?

5. Living in the countryside is less (crowded) _____ than living in a city.

Listening Exercise   Track 50

Listen to the conversation. Then, answer the following questions.

1. (   ) What is Martin's problem?
   (A) He lost his credit cards.
   (B) He was rejected for a loan.
   (C) He is having problems with his car.
   (D) He owes the man a lot of money.

2. (   ) What does the woman suggest about Martin?
   (A) He has a habit of paying bills late.
   (B) He has had trouble with the law before.
   (C) He isn't careful with his credit cards.
   (D) He is usually a responsible person.

3. (   ) What do the police think happened to Martin?
   (A) A thief broke into his house.
   (B) He was the victim of a violent crime.
   (C) His identity was stolen.
   (D) Somebody took his wallet.

Listening Activity 🔘 Track 51

Listen to the report. Then, fill in the information in the chart.

1. What city is the woman reporting on?	
2. How many victims of identity theft were there last year?	
3. What did the thieves usually do?	
4. What was the average amount of money stolen per crime?	
5. How many thieves were caught last year?	

Discussion Questions

1. Have you ever had your wallet or purse stolen? What did you do when you found out?

2. Is paying in cash safer than using a credit card? Why or why not?

3. Should we try to be very careful about giving out information? Or, is it too much trouble to worry about?

Discussion Activity

Thieves often call people on the phone to steal their information. Sometimes they pretend to give away prizes. Sometimes they pretend to be with a company. Working in pairs, practice role playing this kind of phone call.

Example: **Thief**: Congratulations! You won a prize.
Victim: Really? That's great! How do I get it?
Thief: First, I need to know your name and address....

Discuss these questions in pairs.

1. What are some countries with fast-growing economies?

2. Do countries with large populations have any advantages over smaller countries?

3. What problems do poor countries face?

Consider the Topic Read each statement. Check if you agree or disagree with it.

	agree	disagree
1. India will soon be one of the world's largest economies.	☐	☐
2. English is important for international business.	☐	☐
3. Every country has big problems that need solving.	☐	☐

Reading Passage Track 52

1   In recent years, India has **gone through** very big changes. More and more foreign companies are **investing** in the country. And, more and more local companies are growing into world leaders. Indeed, India is quickly **becoming** one of the world's biggest economies.

5   Since 1994, India's **economy** has grown at around 7% per year. In 2007, it was already the world's 10th largest. Many people think it will keep **rising**, to 3rd or 4th place within 10   20 years.

India has several key advantages. First, it has a large and young **population**. So, the country has no problem finding workers for any job. 15   Second, India has a strong service sector. In areas like software and communications, it's getting stronger and stronger. Third, English is one of the country's national languages. 20   That's a big help when doing business **overseas**.

However, India is also **dealing with** many problems. About 20% of the people are **poor**. Plus, a lot needs to be done to improve **education** and health care. These problems are especially big in rural 25   areas.

Over the next few decades, India will have to **come up with** answers to these problems. If it can, and if its economy keeps growing, we'll definitely hear a lot more about the country in the coming years.

---

¹⁵ service sector – businesses that sell services (for example, banking)
¹⁹ national language – official government language
²⁴ rural – in the countryside
²⁶ decade – period of 10 years

Questions about the Reading   Choose the best answer.

1. (   ) What is the main idea?
   (A) Poor countries like India face many different problems.
   (B) India's economy may soon be one of the world's largest.
   (C) Rural areas in India need more help than India's cities.
   (D) India's population is an important reason for its growth.

2. (   ) How do a lot of people feel about India's economy?
   (A) The 7% per year growth rate can't continue.
   (B) It won't go higher than its 2007 ranking.
   (C) In 20 years, it will be stronger than the USA's.
   (D) It may become the world's 3rd largest.

3. (   ) What is suggested about India's service sector?
   (A) It may soon be a key area.
   (B) It is already very important.
   (C) It is not a strong point.
   (D) It is hurt by the large population.

4. (   ) Which of the following is NOT a challenge facing India?
   (A) A large number of poor people
   (B) A serious problem with health care
   (C) A small number of English speakers
   (D) A need to improve education

5. (   ) What does the phrase *coming years* in line 28 mean?
   (A) Near future
   (B) Far away time
   (C) Present time
   (D) Recent past

Writing about the Article   Answer each question based on the article.

1. How did India's economy rank in 2007?

   In 2007, India's economy _____ .

2. Why is it helpful to have a large population?

   With a large population, _____ .

3. What does India need to do over the next several decades?

   India needs to _____ .

Vocabulary Building — Choose the best word to fill in each blank.

1. Craig's family is _____. They don't have money for nice clothes.
   (A) poor   (B) local   (C) rural   (D) young

2. Food prices are _____ all the time. It's one reason I always eat at home.
   (A) growing   (B) rising   (C) getting   (D) finding

3. The _____ is in bad shape. A lot of people are out of work.
   (A) economy   (B) software   (C) decade   (D) advantage

4. If you want to _____ a doctor, you have to study hard.
   (A) think   (B) improve   (C) grow   (D) become

5. In some countries, getting a university _____ is very expensive.
   (A) answer   (B) education   (C) language   (D) leader

6. Before you _____ money in a company, you should learn everything about it.
   (A) invest   (B) hear   (C) think   (D) rise

7. I want to go _____ to study computers. Where would you recommend?
   (A) world   (B) country   (C) overseas   (D) foreign

8. Our country has a large _____, so the cities are very crowded.
   (A) business   (B) population   (C) people   (D) change

Phrase Building — Write the correct phrase in each blank. (Remember to use the correct word form.)

● deal with   ● go through   ● more and more   ● come up with

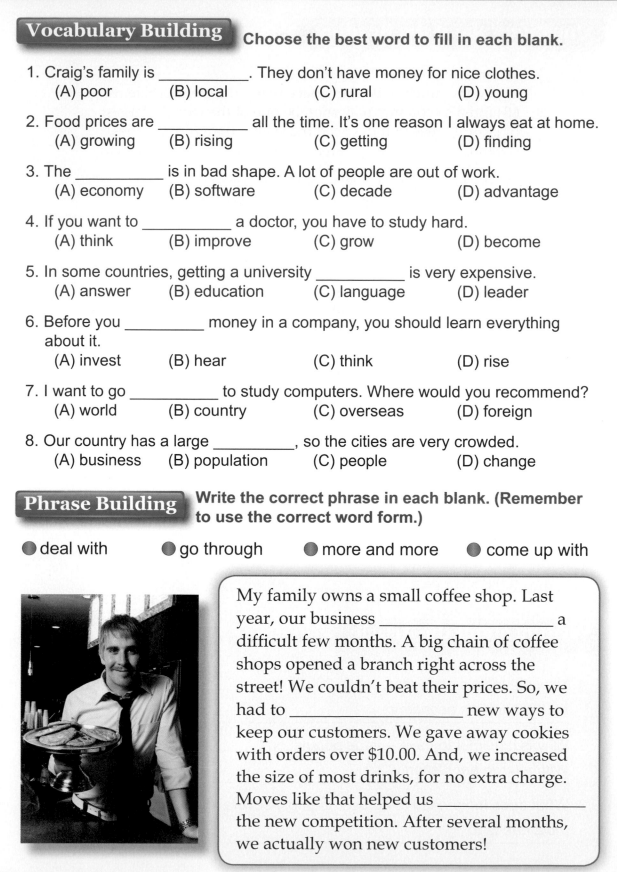

My family owns a small coffee shop. Last year, our business _____ a difficult few months. A big chain of coffee shops opened a branch right across the street! We couldn't beat their prices. So, we had to _____ new ways to keep our customers. We gave away cookies with orders over $10.00. And, we increased the size of most drinks, for no extra charge. Moves like that helped us _____ the new competition. After several months, we actually won new customers!

Grammar Exercise

Adverbs

Complete each sentence with so, however, **or** also.

Example: It rained all day. _____, we stayed inside.
Answer: It rained all day. *So*, we stayed inside.

1. Carl is a very small guy. _____, he is very strong.

2. We want to buy some CDs. _____, we want to go to the pet store.

3. I love science. _____, it's not my strongest subject.

4. The flight and hotel were cheap. _____, we booked a trip to India.

5. Lydia has a beautiful voice. _____, she's a great dancer.

Listening Exercise   Track 53

Listen to the conversation. Then, answer the following questions.

1. (   ) What are the people discussing?
   (A) Taking a trip to India
   (B) Investing in India
   (C) Buying products from India
   (D) Visiting customers in India

2. (   ) Why does the woman favor opening a branch office?
   (A) It's a cheaper way to do business.
   (B) It's the safest way to enter the market.
   (C) It's the only way to learn about customers.
   (D) It's a fast way to get information.

3. (   ) How does the man feel about India's future?
   (A) Hopeful
   (B) Worried
   (C) Confused
   (D) Surprised

Listening Activity ◉ Track 54

Listen to the report. Then, fill in the information in the chart.

1. What was set up in Delhi, India?	
2. How many businesses are taking part?	
3. What country are the companies from?	
4. What fields are the companies in?	
5. What is the yearly cost per company?	

Discussion Questions

1. Which countries will have the biggest economies in 30 years? Will that make the world very different from the way it is now?

2. Do rich countries have a responsibility to help poor countries? Why or why not?

3. Some countries with big populations are very crowded. What should be done in those countries? Is it the government's job to solve the problem?

Discussion Activity

Thinking about your country, consider these four areas: education, health care, public safety, and the economy. Choose the two that you think need the most help. What would you do to improve them?

Example: I think public safety and the economy need the most help. There are some parts of my city that are unsafe to walk through....

Pre-Reading Questions

Discuss these questions in pairs.

1. Do you like to eat junk food? What kinds?

2. What food ingredients are bad for us?

3. What are some good ways to stay healthy?

Consider the Topic

Read each statement. Check if you agree or disagree with it.

	agree	disagree
1. I like eating at fast food restaurants.	☐	☐
2. I read ingredient labels before buying packaged food.	☐	☐
3. The government should make companies sell healthier food.	☐	☐

Reading Passage 🔘 Track 55

1   Sometimes, things that make food taste good are very bad for us. We know that eating too much sugar and salt is unhealthy. Doctors now say trans fat may be a **dangerous** food **ingredient**. There is a **huge** push to **ban** its use.

5   Trans fat is used to prepare many kinds of food. It adds flavor and helps food last longer. It also makes food like cookies and french fries crunchy. However, doctors say it raises our bad cholesterol level. That can cause health problems like heart disease.

  People are **fighting back**. Cities like New York and Philadelphia
10 have banned the use of trans fat in restaurants. Also, fast food chains like KFC and McDonald's are **removing** trans fat from their **products**. They're **replacing** it with healthier ingredients like soybean oil.

  Products sold in supermarkets are also
15 changing. In some countries, companies must list a product's trans fat **amount** on the label. Many packages proudly display (in large letters) that they have "0 Trans Fat."

20   Doctors will be happy to see the end of trans fat in our diets. However, they still **insist on** two important points. First, eating too much of other types of fat can also be unhealthy. Second, **no matter what** you eat, exercise is important to stay healthy.

---

⁵ flavor – taste
⁷ crunchy – making a crunching sound when you eat it
¹¹ chain – type of store with branches in different places
¹⁷ label – part of a product's package with information on it
²⁰ diet – the kinds of food that we eat

Questions about the Reading   Choose the best answer.

1. (   ) What is the main idea?
   (A) People need to exercise to stay healthy.
   (B) Several cities are banning trans fat.
   (C) There are many ways to avoid getting sick.
   (D) Trans fat, though tasty, is unhealthy.

2. (   ) Why are many foods made with trans fat?
   (A) Most other kinds of fat are banned.
   (B) Companies are required by law to do so.
   (C) It is cheaper than all others types of fat.
   (D) Food made with trans fat may last longer.

3. (   ) What are cities like Philadelphia doing about trans fat?
   (A) They are banning all restaurants from using it.
   (B) They are trying to get supermarket labels changed.
   (C) They are making some restaurants list trans fat amounts.
   (D) They are thinking about new laws to limit its use.

4. (   ) Which of the following is NOT true?
   (A) Healthy people do more than just avoid trans fat.
   (B) All products in supermarkets now have zero trans fat.
   (C) In New York, restaurants may not cook with trans fat.
   (D) Eating trans fat leads to higher bad cholesterol levels.

5. (   ) What does the word *level* in line 8 mean?
   (A) amount
   (B) stage
   (C) even
   (D) flat

Writing about the Article   Answer each question based on the article.

1. What can happen if someone's bad cholesterol level is high?

   It can lead to _____.

2. What are fast food restaurants replacing trans fat with?

   They are replacing _____.

3. Besides trans fat, what else do doctors say is unhealthy?

   It is also unhealthy to _____.

Vocabulary Building Choose the best word to fill in each blank.

1. Can you help me _____ the broken light bulb? I can't reach that high up.
   (A) list   (B) replace   (C) display   (D) add

2. It's _____ to drive so fast on a mountain road.
   (A) proud   (B) healthy   (C) dangerous   (D) important

3. What a sweet dessert! Sugar must be its main _____.
   (A) diet   (B) label   (C) fat   (D) ingredient

4. After several accidents, the school decided to _____ playing ball near the classrooms.
   (A) ban   (B) cause   (C) prepare   (D) raise

5. Chocolate chip cookies are the bakery's top-selling _____.
   (A) chains   (B) products   (C) levels   (D) restaurants

6. This sofa is _____. How are we going to fit it through the door?
   (A) huge   (B) proud   (C) happy   (D) unhealthy

7. The total _____ of money I spent on the trip was more than $2,000.
   (A) exercise   (B) type   (C) amount   (D) flavor

8. I have _____ everything from the room. Now we can turn it into a study.
   (A) raised   (B) removed   (C) lasted   (D) caused

Phrase Building Write the correct phrase in each blank. (Remember to use the correct word form.)

● insist on   ● no matter what   ● too much   ● fight back

After doing nothing about its rat problem for years, the city is finally _____.
Every night, a special team of workers goes out looking for rats. They use special cages to catch them. Since rats can be dangerous, the city workers _____ doing everything themselves. They don't want residents to help them. If people see rats in an area, they can call a special number. The "Rat Team" will handle the problem. _____, residents should not try to catch the rats themselves.

Grammar Exercise

Noun Clauses

Complete each sentence with *that*, *what*, or *where*.

Example: He told me _____ he would be here soon.
Answer: He told me *that* he would be here soon.

1. I'm pretty sure _____ the store is closed.

2. Can you tell me _____ the library is?

3. We've decided _____ the game should be canceled.

4. I don't understand _____ this note is trying to say.

5. I'll find out _____ the noise is coming from.

Listening Exercise Track 56

Listen to the conversation. Then, answer the following questions.

1. (   ) Where are the people?
   (A) At a school
   (B) At a supermarket
   (C) At a hospital
   (D) At a restaurant

2. (   ) Why does the man need to be careful about what he eats?
   (A) He wants to lose weight.
   (B) He read a report about trans fat.
   (C) He and his wife are both on a diet.
   (D) He received doctor's orders.

3. (   ) What will the man probably eat for dessert?
   (A) Cake
   (B) Ice cream
   (C) Fruit
   (D) Pie

Listening Activity Track 57

Listen to the report. Then, fill in the information in the chart.

1. Where were people asked about trans fat?	
2. How many people answered questions?	
3. What percentage of people choose food with less trans fat?	
4. What percentage of people want to learn more?	
5. How can people find trans fat free food?	

Discussion Questions

1. Why do children love fast food restaurants (like McDonald's) so much?

2. Some people say life is short, and we should eat whatever makes us happy. Do you agree or disagree?

3. These days, we have a lot of information about how to eat right and stay healthy. However, many people ignore that information and live unhealthy lives. Why is that?

Discussion Activity

Some companies' products are full of trans fat. Should they have to pay the medical bills of people who get sick from eating too much trans fat? In groups of four, hold a mini debate, with two classmates on each side. Spend a few minutes considering the reasons for your point of view. Then hold the mini debate.

Example: Our side feels companies should not have to pay the health care bills. People can decide what they want to eat. They should be responsible for their own lives....

Discuss these questions in pairs.

1. How often do you use a computer?

2. What tasks are computers very good at?

3. Should we be afraid of robots becoming too smart?

Consider the Topic

Read each statement. Check if you agree or disagree with it.

	agree	disagree
1. Computers make our lives easier.	☐	☐
2. It would be interesting to work with a robot.	☐	☐
3. I would like to have a robot pet.	☐	☐

Reading Passage   Track 58

1   Intelligent machines are a part of our daily lives. They **handle** Internet searches, talk to us on the phone, and plan **schedules** for companies. These machines all use some kind of Artificial Intelligence (AI).

5   AI is the power of machines to **carry out** intelligent jobs. The term was first used in 1956 by scientists at Dartmouth University. They were interested in programming computers to **think** like people.

    That's **easier said than done**. In movies like *I, Robot*, we often see thinking machines. They're very smart and can do almost anything

10   people can. Of course, the real world is quite different. It's not yet **possible** to build computers with brains like ours.

    However, we can program machines to be good at **certain skills**. For example, in 1997, a supercomputer beat the world's best chess player. Eight years later, several robot cars finished a race across a

15   desert. Also, many computer games have **built-in** AI to make them more exciting.

    And that's just the **beginning**. In the **future**, computers with AI will handle many more jobs. They'll

20   help out at banks, stores, and police departments. Also, expect to see more robots (like Sony's AIBO) that use AI. All these changes will make the world a very different, yet very

25   interesting place.

---

¹ intelligent – smart
¹³ supercomputer – very fast (and usually very large) computer
²¹ expect – believe that something will happen

Questions about the Reading
Choose the best answer.

1. (   ) What does the article suggest about intelligent machines?
      (A) They are programmed by computers.
      (B) Many of them are made at Dartmouth University.
      (C) Only scientists are interested in them.
      (D) We have worked on them for more than 50 years.

2. (   ) How are thinking machines often shown in movies?
      (A) They are unlike real-world robots.
      (B) They sometimes have more than one brain.
      (C) They are not as smart as today's machines.
      (D) They usually fight against people.

3. (   ) What are computers still unable to do?
      (A) Drive cars across a desert
      (B) Beat excellent chess players
      (C) Think the same way as people
      (D) Play computer games well

4. (   ) What does the word *term* in line 5 mean?
      (A) phrase
      (B) length
      (C) period
      (D) rule

5. (   ) What does the article suggest about the future?
      (A) The world will be a very dangerous place.
      (B) Robots will help people in many fields.
      (C) Computers will handle all of our work.
      (D) Sony's AIBO will be a best-selling item.

Writing about the Article
Answer each question based on the article.

1. These days, what can intelligent machines do?
   They can _____ .

2. What were scientists at Dartmouth University interested in?
   They were interested in _____ .

3. Where will intelligent machines help out in the future?
   They will be used at _____ .

Vocabulary Building
Choose the best word to fill in each blank.

1. It's not an easy question. I need to _____ about how to answer it.
   (A) expect   (B) finish   (C) think   (D) use

2. Be careful where you walk around. _____ parts of the city are dangerous.
   (A) Interested   (B) Certain   (C) Intelligent   (D) Real

3. We arrived late, so we missed the _____ of the show.
   (A) beginning   (B) anything   (C) machine   (D) place

4. I can fix almost any watch. It's a _____ I learned from my father.
   (A) department   (B) computer   (C) change   (D) skill

5. You're working 60 hours a week. How can you _____ that much work?
   (A) beat   (B) build   (C) make   (D) handle

6. It's not _____ to fit everything inside. The car is too small.
   (A) exciting   (B) different   (C) possible   (D) daily

7. My _____ for next week is full. I have meetings every day.
   (A) world   (B) schedule   (C) race   (D) brain

8. In the _____, it may be common to talk to robots. These days, few robots can hold a conversation.
   (A) power   (B) player   (C) future   (D) scientist

Phrase Building
Write the correct phrase in each blank.

● carry out   ● easier said than done   ● part of   ● built-in

Larry designs products for a home electronics company. Last July, his boss asked him to _____ a special job. He wanted Larry to design a mirror with a _____ clock timer. Larry thought it was strange, but he worked hard on the project. Designing it was _____. It took him several months. After Larry was done, he asked his boss about the product's use. "Simple," his boss answered, "I tell my children they spend half the day in front of the mirror. Now I can prove it!"

Grammar Exercise

Adjectives: -ed vs. -ing

Choose the correct form of the word.

Example: Wasn't that an (interested/interesting) movie?
Answer: Wasn't that an (interested/(interesting)) movie?

1. Gary was really (excited/exciting) to get your e-mail.

2. The (bored/boring) play made me fall asleep.

3. Painting the whole house sounds like a (tired/tiring) job.

4. I was (surprised/surprising) to hear the news about Hiro.

5. This (confused/confusing) map is going to get us lost!

Listening Exercise Track 59

Listen to the conversation. Then, answer the following questions.

1. (　) Where are the people?
    (A) At a science museum
    (B) At a training camp
    (C) At a robot factory
    (D) At a language school

2. (　) Who is Mr. Santos?
    (A) The man's friend
    (B) A robot designer
    (C) An electronics teacher
    (D) Lisa's supervisor

3. (　) What is the man surprised about?
    (A) Being allowed inside
    (B) Seeing Mr. Santos there
    (C) Speaking with a machine
    (D) Hearing Lisa's big secret

Listening Activity 🔘 Track 60

Listen to the report. Then, fill in the information in the chart.

1. What is the report about?	
2. What do doctors use to help them?	
3. What are robots able to perform?	
4. Why are robots good at their jobs?	
5. What may robots do in the future?	

Discussion Questions

1. Imagine you could own an intelligent robot. What tasks would you have it do for you?

2. In the movies, intelligent robots are often dangerous or even violent. If we make robots too smart, will they fight against us one day?

3. Every year, computers are getting smarter and faster. In your opinion, is this a good thing, a bad thing, or both?

Discussion Activity

Imagine the world 200 years from now. Working with several classmates, decide what it will be like. How important will robots be? What will they do for us? (Or, will we work for them?) After each group comes up with its vision of the future, share it with the class.

Example: In 200 years, there will be robots everywhere. They will look just like people, dogs, horses, and every other animal. And, they'll all speak, in any language you want....

Target Word List

☐ advantage	Unit 15	☐ consider	Unit 14
☐ afford	Unit 1	☐ contact	Unit 2
☐ afterwards	Unit 8	☐ contain	Unit 6
☐ agree	Unit 14	☐ convenient	Unit 6
☐ amazing	Unit 8	☐ creative	Unit 5
☐ amount	Unit 19	☐ crime	Unit 17
☐ anymore	Unit 3	☐ culture	Unit 9
☐ art	Unit 5	☐ dangerous	Unit 19
☐ Asia	Unit 13	☐ design	Unit 10
☐ attention	Unit 11	☐ direction	Unit 5
☐ attract	Unit 3	☐ discuss	Unit 2
☐ ban	Unit 19	☐ divide	Unit 6
☐ become	Unit 18	☐ Earth	Unit 8
☐ beginning	Unit 20	☐ economy	Unit 18
☐ benefit	Unit 4	☐ education	Unit 18
☐ besides	Unit 15	☐ elsewhere	Unit 10
☐ build	Unit 15	☐ employee	Unit 4
☐ cash	Unit 17	☐ energy	Unit 14
☐ cause	Unit 14	☐ enjoy	Unit 10
☐ century	Unit 12	☐ entertainment	Unit 3
☐ certain	Unit 20	☐ environment	Unit 1
☐ challenge	Unit 14	☐ equal	Unit 12
☐ change	Unit 8	☐ even	Unit 7
☐ chat	Unit 12	☐ event	Unit 12
☐ clean	Unit 14	☐ exciting	Unit 3
☐ clinic	Unit 1	☐ expert	Unit 17
☐ collect	Unit 10	☐ famous	Unit 5
☐ common	Unit 16	☐ fashionable	Unit 7
☐ community	Unit 1	☐ field	Unit 10

☐ foreign	Unit 9		☐ museum	Unit 13
☐ form	Unit 1		☐ native	Unit 11
☐ fortunately	Unit 9		☐ necessary	Unit 17
☐ future	Unit 20		☐ novel	Unit 6
☐ generous	Unit 1		☐ offer	Unit 7
☐ government	Unit 14		☐ official	Unit 11
☐ handle	Unit 20		☐ online	Unit 3
☐ healthy	Unit 2		☐ organize	Unit 1
☐ hobby	Unit 2		☐ overseas	Unit 18
☐ holiday	Unit 11		☐ owner	Unit 7
☐ host	Unit 13		☐ paint	Unit 5
☐ however	Unit 17		☐ personal	Unit 17
☐ huge	Unit 19		☐ plan	Unit 8
☐ illegal	Unit 5		☐ pollution	Unit 4
☐ immigrant	Unit 11		☐ poor	Unit 18
☐ important	Unit 15		☐ population	Unit 18
☐ improve	Unit 4		☐ possible	Unit 20
☐ include	Unit 2		☐ present	Unit 11
☐ industry	Unit 3		☐ pressure	Unit 16
☐ information	Unit 12		☐ prevent	Unit 17
☐ ingredient	Unit 19		☐ private	Unit 2
☐ invest	Unit 18		☐ product	Unit 19
☐ labor	Unit 11		☐ professional	Unit 10
☐ located	Unit 13		☐ publish	Unit 6
☐ major	Unit 13		☐ quality	Unit 4
☐ member	Unit 2		☐ raise	Unit 16
☐ message	Unit 2		☐ range	Unit 7
☐ method	Unit 12		☐ reason	Unit 16
☐ modern	Unit 10		☐ recommend	Unit 17

☐ reduce	Unit 4	☐ topic	Unit 9
☐ regular	Unit 4	☐ tourist	Unit 8
☐ relative	Unit 16	☐ towards	Unit 16
☐ remove	Unit 19	☐ trade	Unit 13
☐ replace	Unit 19	☐ traditional	Unit 4
☐ resident	Unit 13	☐ transportation	Unit 15
☐ rise	Unit 18	☐ travel	Unit 15
☐ rude	Unit 9	☐ treat	Unit 5
☐ safe	Unit 15	☐ trip	Unit 8
☐ salary	Unit 9	☐ unusual	Unit 16
☐ schedule	Unit 20	☐ view	Unit 7
☐ sensitive	Unit 9	☐ volunteer	Unit 1
☐ service	Unit 7	☐ website	Unit 6
☐ sibling	Unit 16	☐ welcome	Unit 11
☐ simple	Unit 3	☐ worth	Unit 9
☐ single	Unit 12		
☐ skill	Unit 20		
☐ space	Unit 8		
☐ special	Unit 10		
☐ stock	Unit 7		
☐ style	Unit 5		
☐ successful	Unit 6		
☐ support	Unit 13		
☐ swing	Unit 3		
☐ switch	Unit 12		
☐ system	Unit 15		
☐ technology	Unit 6		
☐ temperature	Unit 14		
☐ think	Unit 20		

Target Phrase List

- [ ] above all — Unit 7
- [ ] add up — Unit 16
- [ ] all over — Unit 5
- [ ] along the lines of — Unit 3
- [ ] apply for — Unit 17
- [ ] as much as possible — Unit 17
- [ ] as well as — Unit 15
- [ ] based on — Unit 15
- [ ] believe it or not — Unit 8
- [ ] break into — Unit 17
- [ ] built-in — Unit 20
- [ ] carry out — Unit 20
- [ ] come down — Unit 8
- [ ] come over — Unit 3
- [ ] come up with — Unit 18
- [ ] count on — Unit 1
- [ ] deal with — Unit 18
- [ ] easier said than done — Unit 20
- [ ] far away — Unit 15
- [ ] far from the truth — Unit 4
- [ ] fight back — Unit 19
- [ ] figure out — Unit 2
- [ ] fill out — Unit 12
- [ ] focus on — Unit 3
- [ ] for example — Unit 14
- [ ] form ties with — Unit 1
- [ ] frown on — Unit 9
- [ ] get along with — Unit 11
- [ ] get in touch with — Unit 7
- [ ] go through — Unit 18

- [ ] grow up — Unit 16
- [ ] head to — Unit 8
- [ ] help out — Unit 11
- [ ] in addition — Unit 10
- [ ] in this way — Unit 12
- [ ] insist on — Unit 19
- [ ] keep up with — Unit 2
- [ ] lead to — Unit 14
- [ ] lend a hand — Unit 7
- [ ] look over someone's shoulder — Unit 4
- [ ] no matter what — Unit 19
- [ ] no more than — Unit 6
- [ ] on a large scale — Unit 1
- [ ] on the market — Unit 6
- [ ] on the plus side — Unit 16
- [ ] one at a time — Unit 6
- [ ] over the years — Unit 5
- [ ] pick up — Unit 11
- [ ] pour money into — Unit 13
- [ ] proud of — Unit 13
- [ ] put out — Unit 10
- [ ] seen as — Unit 9
- [ ] set up — Unit 12
- [ ] slow down — Unit 14
- [ ] stay in touch — Unit 2
- [ ] such as — Unit 4
- [ ] take time — Unit 9
- [ ] to name a few — Unit 13
- [ ] top notch — Unit 10
- [ ] worry about — Unit 5

About the Author

Andrew E. Bennett holds an EdM (Master of Education) degree from Harvard University and a BA degree from UC Santa Cruz. He has studied seven languages. It's a life-long passion that began with a study of Spanish and continues with his ongoing studies of Chinese and Japanese.

Andrew has been involved in English education since 1993, both as a teacher and a writer. He has taught a variety of subjects, including English composition, business writing, English literature, and TOEFL preparation.

Andrew is the author of more than 30 English learning books, including classroom texts, supplementary books, self-study books, as well as TOEIC preparation texts. In addition to writing and teaching, he regularly attends ESL conferences and gives presentations to groups of teachers at schools and symposiums.

Central to Andrew's teaching philosophy is an emphasis on content. His work includes subjects from countries around the world, giving his writing an international flavor. Andrew also enjoys writing about cultural issues, as he is convinced of the vital link between language and culture.